FARBER'S
POSTULATES

of

EDUCATION

*A Survival Guide for Teachers
and a Reality Check
for Others*

ROBERT FARBER

Aperture Press

Paperback ISBN: 978-0-9909302-3-5
Library of Congress Control Number: 2015906400

First edition, 2015

Book designed by Stephen Wagner.

Cover images courtesy of Ron Leishman
and Maridav/Tobkatrina/Bigstock.com.

To my wife, Janice,
the most thoughtful and loving person
that I have ever known.

CONTENTS

INTRODUCTION

The purpose of this book is to introduce you to the American education system as it exists, *not to change it*. Many great men and women have tried to change and improve education but with only fleeting effects. The many fine teachers who are in the classrooms make the system work in spite of many obstacles. Unfortunately many young teachers leave the profession after only as few years because they become disillusioned with the system. This is because colleges and universities do not provide a potential teacher with a realistic view of education. Teacher preparation courses present only the idealistic view of education. It appears to me that education professors are afraid that the future teachers would change majors if a true picture of the day to day operation of schools were presented. This is really an insult to the maturity and intelligence of the fine students who are education majors.

There are many concerned parents and citizens who are upset at one aspect or another of education. They can not understand certain things that happen in schools. They wonder why teachers are not doing a better job, or about the issues that are leading to militant teachers' unions but most of all why schools aren't doing a better job.

I have spent over four-and-a-half decades as a classroom teacher in both public and private schools. I have taught middle school, high school and college levels. I've taught in a couple of the worst urban high schools in my state, as well as high schools which were among the nation's best. I have shared my students' joys and sorrows, seen my students succeed and fail in life. I truly looked forward to going to school most days. I enjoyed my students as they discovered science in my classroom. I would tell people that it was hard to believe that I was getting paid to have this much fun.

People, even other teachers thought I was crazy. The fact was that I understood and could ignore the craziness of the "educational system." I didn't waste much time and energy trying to fight or change the system. I focused on helping my students understand the science that I was permitted to teach.

There are very few people who are willing to admit the truth about what makes things happen in education. What makes education work are teachers, not any system or curriculum. There is no magic formula to being a successful teacher. All the education courses in the world will not make a person a teacher. Every teacher has had to take a course called "The Principles of Education." People can have principles, institutions and political systems can not. This book provides a series of postulates by which one can comprehend and operate in the quasi-political system of education.

I have seen many very talented teachers "burn out." They do not burn out because of what happens in their classrooms. They burn out because they become frustrated and disenchanted with the educational system. The model educational system taught by the college of education does not exist. Teachers burn out when they realize the realities and limitations of real educational systems. Each teacher must learn what is possible and not possible in education. They must learn to function in a less than perfect system that has many faces. The sooner that they learn this, the better for them and for education. It is my hope that this book will help them reach this point sooner and without learning everything the hard way. This is what they don't teach in teachers' colleges.

Over my many years in the classroom, I have seen many changes. When I was in school, corporal punishment still was widely practiced. Students were paddled for minor offenses. I was paddled in high school because a teacher suspected me of whispering in study hall. By the time I began teaching, only administrators paddled students. Teachers used to verbally humiliate students.

Fortunately these practices have ended. The pendulum has moved to the other extreme. Now teachers can lose their jobs for touching a student. Many schools prohibit teachers from making any negative comments about a student or the student's work. The pendulum could begin to swing back sometime in the future. Teaching methods have changed from forcing students to memorize things to allowing students to express opinions about things. Machines store and retrieve information and the students now learn to how to deal with the information. The availability of calculators makes a student's inability to do basic math well less of a handicap. Computers that turn speech into written text may make handwriting obsolete. How and what is taught in schools will continue to change. The only thing which is permanent in this world is change. Many people expend much energy resisting change. It is the only thing that humans universally fear because its consequences can not be known with absolute certainty.

What we teach and how we teach in our schools will keep changing. But this little book is not about changes. It is about the constants in the American system of education. The only thing that does not change is human nature. The nature of the humans that make up the educational hierarchy has not and will not change.

One should never take life too seriously. This is especially true for the professional educator. This book is written in this spirit. It is meant to be humorous and informative. It is not a criticism of education but a practical guide how to survive within the system and keep your sanity. The only difference between being "in the groove" and being "in the rut" is your point of view. Hopefully this little book will help you avoid the ruts.

CHAPTER 1

Farber's First Postulate

LOGIC AND INTELLIGENCE HAVE NO PLACE IN EDUCATION

Logic and intelligence have no place in American education. If you are able to accept this fact then all the rest of the educational system will make sense. Now you can become a happy and successful teacher.

First let us define intelligence. We all agree that there is such a thing and that some people are more intelligent than others. The conceptual definitions of intelligence such as "thought power" don't give us anything that we can measure. What we need is an operational definition that provides some measurable parameters by which to judge intelligence.

Is intelligence the ability to read? No, reading is something which is learned and something which improves with practice. We know of many intelligent people who never learned to read or to write in English, French, Spanish or any other language. Reading does not necessarily mean that the person comprehends what is read. And what is reading comprehension? How many of us have had the experience of spending several class periods in a college literature class discussing the meaning of a one-page poem. At the conclusion of this, you realized that the poem meant different things to different people because each person interpreted the poem through their unique life experiences. This experience should give evidence that any measure of reading comprehension will have a bias that will make it invalid.

Is the ability to do math problems a measure of intelligence? We all know that computers can do math problems faster and more accurately than we humans, but computers are not considered intelligent. Most people will agree that the ability to handle numbers or manipulate symbols does not truly define intelligence. Our experience tells us that there are many brilliant people who do not display much math ability.

Does the ability to communicate indicate intelligence? Now we have the problem of the level of communication. Have you tried to communicate with your teenage offspring? How often have you been able to follow the "simple assembly" instructions which may have been written by an engineer? And then there are the instructions for filling out your income tax return! Let's face it, the meanings of words (language) change in different professions, generations, locations, and social groups. Some very bright people need someone else to take their thoughts/ideas and interpret them for others. We can safely conclude that the measure of the ability to communicate is full of pitfalls and is not a good measure of intelligence.

Does creativity indicate intelligence? This would seem a more promising yardstick of intelligence. Once again we have the problem of defining something in terms that we can measure. There are many kinds of creativity and very few types can be objectively evaluated. A visit to an art museum is enough to demonstrate the diversity of creative persons.

The simple fact is that *there is no set of measures that we can agree upon as an absolute measure of intelligence!*

The most widely used and least understood tests in American education are the IQ tests. The Intelligent Quotient test is a measure of something that can not be measured! Most of our educational programs are based on them in some way or other.

So, you think that you missed something? You say that it is illogical to have and to use this test? It does not seem very logical to base so much on this test? You forgot Farber's first postulate of education: *Logic and intelligence have no place in American education.*

—

Let's take a quick look at the history of the IQ test and how it developed. It began with Alfred Binet early in this century. He started with a definition of "normal" to be anything that 65% to 75% of the children of a particular age could do successfully. This definition requires 25 percent of the children to be classified as subnormal. He developed his standards for the "normal" by testing 200 Paris school children who ranged in age from three to fifteen years. He established what tasks could normally be accomplished by a child of each age thus the test could measure the "mental age" of a child. The test was then given to some children in California, but the results came out different. Some professors from Stanford University took on the job of revising and improving the test. They developed the idea of "intelligent quotient." This was defined as "mental age as measured by the test, divided by child's actual age." This fraction was then multiplied by 100.

$$\frac{\text{Mental Age}}{\text{Chronological Age}} \times 100 = \text{Intelligence Quotient}$$

Education works on the assumption that IQ does not change as a child grows and learns. If we used such a formula to rate the physical development of a child would, we adhere to this assumption?

$$\frac{\text{Physical Maturity}}{\text{Chronological Age}} \times 100 = \text{Physical Development Quotient}$$

We are aware that children develop physically at different rates. Everyone can cite examples of the skinny little boy who was pushed around in junior high school who grew into a tall muscular athletic star or the homely wallflower who became the beauty queen. So why are we so willing to believe that the ratio between mental development and chronological age will not change? But this is education—logic does not apply.

Binet devised this test originally to divide children into three categories-above average, normal and below normal. Fifty percent of the children would be classified as normal, twenty-five percent would be above average, and twenty five percent would be below normal. Now with the number scale it was mathematically possible to make over a hundred categories.

What happens if you give a child the IQ test once a month for the school year? Will the score always be the same? Of course we all realize that the score will vary, so the question now is how much will it vary? Now we must apply some statistical theory to determine the "standard error" of the test. The modern form of the test is said to have a standard error of 4 points. This is what the company that sells the test admits to, which is great if you *believe* every sales pitch you hear. (Most educators were born yesterday.) This means that, *normally,* the score received by a child will be within 4 points of the score that this child will receive next month. This means that if a child is given a single test and scores 90, his or her actual IQ could be as high as 94 or as low as 86.

This assumes that the child is normal. There is always the possibility that this child is one of the exceptions whose test variations will not fall into the "standard" test errors. What if the child was ill or had an emotional upset on the day the test was given?[1] What if the child just did not try since the test did not count as a grade? At this point the single test score is invalid.

So now we give this test to almost every American school child. It is a copyrighted booklet with computerized scoring. The school purchases it from one of several competing educational supply companies. In most cases the test is given once in the elementary school years and that single score becomes the student's *permanent* IQ on the student's permanent record. A large part of the direction of his/her education will be determined by this number.

—

1   With the divorce rate, crime on the streets, drugs, etc we see many more children coming to school with emotional problems.

As a first year teacher I had the lower ability children. (All new teachers are normally given the classes that the other teachers don't want to teach.) Being young, idealistic, and inexperienced, I thought that my job was to bring my students to higher levels of thinking and to motivate them to attempt more challenging courses. I was successful and had a couple of students with all A's and B's. At the mid-term meeting of the teachers who taught the eleventh grade, I recommended that these students be moved to the next higher academic track. The vice principal immediately whipped out the student's permanent record cards and told me that these students did not have the IQ to work on a higher level. In one case, the student's IQ was *two points* below the cut off for the higher track. I tried to argue about test deviation only to be told that I was out of order and that as I gained more experience I would understand these things.

Years later I taught the top section of science. I had a couple of students who were not doing well. I checked with several of their other teachers and found that these students were not doing very well in most subjects. I went to the administration and suggested that these students be transferred to a less challenging section where they would find the work easier. Guess what? The permanent record cards came up on a screen, and I was told that these students had high IQs and could do the work. They would not be transferred to another section. They must work up to their ability or repeat the course.

This proves that I am a slow learner since these two incidents occurred twenty six years, six educational reform movements, dozens of curriculum revisions, and countless school reorganizations apart.

—

Let's look at the typical school year. Imagine yourself as a student teacher or a first year teacher trying to understand and function effectively in an urban school. The school year begins with almost 40 students assigned to each class. The teachers' contract states that there shall not be more than

33 students in a class. This is not a new contract clause; it has existed for decades. Why, you ask, do school administrators set up a program with 40 students per class?

Logical question. Well, let's look at the possibilities. Maybe they expected a lot of students to drop out or transfer to other schools. This sounds reasonable except, when you inquire further, you discover that this overloading of classes happens every year. So, you ask, don't they learn from experience? The schools obviously did not learn from previous experience.

Intelligence has often been defined as the ability to learn from experience. So if you apply Farber's first postulate, *Logic and intelligence has no place in education,* you find that everything begins to make sense.

Another interesting question is why do they design the lab-lecture room for only 24 students when the teachers' contract allows for 33 students per class and the roster office assigned 40 students to this room?

Or why do they build a school in the inner city with 28 outside entrances/exits that provide any and every bum, drug dealer, sex fiend, or mass murderer easy access? It would take 28 paid security aides to secure this school. In addition, it is a violation of the fire code to lock these doors which students continuously open via panic bars to let all sorts of people admission into the school.

As another extreme example, a public high school in my city has a street through the middle of the building that allows drug dealers and others a drive through access to the building.

You were told that you were lucky to be assigned to this new modern building. Although it is in the middle of a ghetto, it was designed and built to be an ideal school for an ideal community (which is somewhere in Kansas.) You could have been unlucky enough to be assigned one of those old school buildings which are built like a fortress with only a couple of entrances. These buildings are easily monitored. Of course you can see the logic of this. OOPS, logic has no place in education. If you persist in looking for the logic of the system, you will be driven to distraction.

Now you are ready to hand out textbooks and get down to the business of teaching. Whoops, I forgot to tell you that we are not allowed to hand out books until the class sizes are reduced to 33 students per class. At least 50% of your students will have schedule changes and will be moved to another science class. Whenever a student is moved out of one class period into another, his/her whole schedule of classes is subject to change. This roster hopscotch will continue for months. It will be about six to eight weeks before you will be allowed to issue books.

The students know better than you who will have a schedule change and they don't need to do much work in your class since they know they may be leaving. They may even be disruptive. They also can count on the fact that you will not be the one grading them, which, limits your authority. This does not set the tone that you wanted for your classes. Yes, learning will be at a slower rate until classes are reduced and books are issued.

This is the age of computers. Why does it take so long to reschedule the students? I can tell that you have never dealt with government agencies before this. You will soon learn about forms and procedures.

The school district does not have enough teachers to reduce class size to the maximum size allowed by union contract and must hire more teachers. This takes some time. The district makes this same mistake every year but will not admit it until October, when it becomes evident to even the dullest administrative drone or the tightest school board director that there is no other way to reduce the class size to the contract maximum[2] without hiring additional teachers. This rostering system may not be sound educational policy, but it is the way schools operate.

After four or five weeks of duplicating and handing out materials to students who do not have text books to read, study, or do homework exercises, you receive a memo telling you that you must conserve paper. You are reminded that paper is purchased once for the year and the school has already

---

2   The typical urban school district needs to hire a hundred or more new teachers each year. Figure the money saved if hiring is delayed one month. One ninth of all those salaries and benefits is a lot of money.

used almost half of the paper allotment. This memo is three pages long.

About five weeks into the school year you are told that it is time to write failure warning reports for each and every student who *might fail* your course. These reports are to be turned in to your department head who will check them and then forward them to the school office. The people at the office will sort them according to the student's homeroom. The reports will then be sent to the homeroom advisor who will put them in envelopes and address and seal the envelopes. They will be returned to the school office. The school office will send them to the district office to be stamped and mailed. This process takes about two weeks, which means that the failure warnings are delivered to the students' homes about five days before the first quarter (9 week) when grades are due. During the time that you are writing these reports the students' classes are rescheduled and the class size is reduced to the contractual maximum. This means that many of these failing students are no longer in your class.

Now when the parents call to find out what they can do to help their child pass your course you can give them one of the following answers:

1. I no longer have your child in my class so you need to talk to the new teacher. (We are not usually informed who the new teacher will be, or who taught the student who just rescheduled into the class.)
2. The report period is over in just three more days. It is too late to significantly improve your child's grade at this time.

You ask, "Is this helping the student? Is this helping the parents? Is this good public relations?"

The obvious answer is "no!" It creates ill will all around and gives the parents a negative opinion of the teachers and the school system. It makes the public anti-teacher. We have all been on the receiving end of the recent wave of teacher bashing.

So why do it?

You're being logical again—how many times do I have to tell you that logic is not used in education?

—

As you were writing the "failure warning" reports, you noticed that there was an unusually high failure rate in your first period class. The reason seems fairly obvious to you. Many students come to school late every day, and all during the first period, late students straggle into the classroom. You must stop the lesson and check that they have a late pass. Then the student, being a typical adolescent, gives a "hi" sign to their friends and slowly settles into a seat. This process is repeated a half dozen times in every first period class.

In many schools the teacher is now required to put the gradebook online. If the gradebook is on line, why are teachers required to write and mail home so many grade reports?

You also notice that the homeroom/advisory period is in the middle of the morning. Now you again try to apply some logic to improve the educational process. Why not have the homeroom/advisory period first thing in the morning and thus prevent the disruptions in first period caused by lateness? Fewer students would miss class and the overall educational process would be improved.

Again logic does not apply to the situation. Logic tells you that education is more important than homeroom/advisory. Homeroom or advisory is when we take the *official* daily attendance and the principal wants this school to look good. The highest percentage of students in attendance is in the middle of the morning so that is when advisory period is scheduled. In some states and school systems, school funding is based on the daily attendance of the students rather than on the number of students enrolled in the school. Education is not an administrative priority; it is the teacher's problem and responsibility. If you suggest changing schedule, you will be told that it is *your* job to motivate students to get to school and class on time. If there is a problem, it is *your* problem, not the school's problem.

If you are at the middle or high school level, you are aware of a growing absentee rate as the year progresses. You find that it is difficult to teach students who are not physically in the class. Some students miss two or three days every week. You have written volumes of absence reports and nothing has changed.

The truth is that dozens of trees have already sacrificed their very lives to produce that paper already used on each of these students. If you don't continue writing reports, you will be negligent in your duties as a teacher. Only yesterday did I read that my local state representative said the "low attendance in our schools is shameful" and that "something should be done about it." In truth, most state attendance laws have no teeth and to "do something" takes hours of hearings and lots of legal fees so you really MUST keeping writing those cards and letters. I'm not joking. It is called "CYA"(covering your ass) and successful educators spend a lot of time doing CYA paperwork.

Logic tells you that education is the primary function of the school system and that the poor attendance problems will be addressed at a higher level in the near future. Again logic does not work. The primary function of school is day care. People need and want someplace to send and someone to supervise their children every day. Let the school close for a heating problem or because of bad road conditions. You only need to go to shopping malls or supermarkets and listen to people complain about the inconvenience of having *their* children at home. Listen carefully to the people who advocate year 'round school and you will discover that what they really want is for someone else to be responsible for their children in the summer. Let any school board institute strict academic standards or attendance minimums for promotion and watch the public outcry of how unfair it is to hold their children to an *arbitrary standard* or an *abstract norm*. The school directors either back down quickly or are voted out of office.

—

If you thought that education is illogical at this point, you haven't seen anything yet. Just wait until to the end of the school year. In my school system "final exams" are given three weeks before the end of the school year. The students are to take their final exams and then attend for another two weeks. It is obvious to even the dullest students that the course ends with the final exam. If the course is over why attend class for another two weeks? At this point, only Farber's first postulate and the 180 day attendance law apply.

What do the teachers and students do in school for two weeks after the end of final exams. There is always a memo from the district office directing the teachers to continue "meaningful education" but from a student's point of view, very little in school is meaningful unless it adds or detracts from their grade. Since their grades are already turned in for the school year, the students find little reason to cooperate with the teacher or even come to class.

However this is only part of the story. The teachers in my school have been required some years to inform the high school office which students will pass and which students will fail their course a week *before* the final exams are given. Once this is turned in to the office no changes are permitted. However, under special circumstances, a failing mark may be changed to a passing mark. Seniors, who may not graduate due to course failures were exempt. It is always costly to have a student repeat a year. The reverse is not allowed!

I thought that this system was ridiculous. I discovered that several other school principals in our district require the teachers to enter the students' final *numerical* grades before the final exams are given.

A teacher without knowledge of Farber's first postulate may ask how one can *logically* do this before giving and grading the final exams? The teacher naive enough to ask such a logical question will be rewarded with that condescending look reserved for very new teachers or very dull people and told that "by this time of the year a *"good"* teacher would now know the students well enough to be able to accurately predict these things." If you dare follow this thought to its logical conclusion, a *"very good"* teacher could have predicted those who would pass and those who would fail by the end of January. We could have ended the school year then and saved the tax payers a pile of money and ourselves the hassle of the second half of the school year. Once more, logic has no place in education.

If this sounds unbelievable, you must remember that everyone who works for the school system wants to leave for summer recess at the same time. If the teachers turned in grades, etc. the last day of school, the computer operators and office staff would have to work another week or two in order to process grades, complete next year's student rosters, etc.

—

As a new teacher, you may have noticed that many veteran teachers have brought electric heaters and fans to school This is because the school is a computerized climate controlled building with windows that do not open except maybe for one small pane.[3] You will soon discover that bringing in your own heater and fan is a personal survival tactic. When the air conditioning is on, some classrooms could double as meat lockers. The teachers keep an electric heater under their desk to keep from freezing. When the heating system is on, the opposite is true. In sub-freezing weather many classrooms reach 90 degrees with the "windows" open and some teachers are using the electric fans that they brought in from home to cool their classroom.

You may approach the principal with the logic that it is wasteful of the school budget not to control excess heating and cooling. Your logic does not apply. Energy use does not affect the *school's* budget; rather it comes out of the district energy budget. Any saving in the energy budget

---

3   I think that this small window was installed so that kids could shout out at their friends on the street, commit auditory assault on citizens foolish enough to walk by a school, and to pass weapons and drugs, etc. into the school building.

will not be given to the school budget.

In large school districts the principal has no authority over the building's custodian. In order to get the heat or air conditioning adjusted correctly, the principal must contact an assistant superintendent for instruction, who will pass the complaint to the assistant superintendent for engineering and maintenance who will contact the district engineering department who will tell the custodian to adjust the climate control system. Did you get all that?

Let me put it in simple terms. The principal has no authority over the school custodian. He or she can not direct or order the custodian to do anything. The principal can not hire, fire, demote, transfer or directly interfere with the activities or non-activities of the custodian. The school district administrative organization is based on Farber's first postulate and, therefore, this all makes perfect sense.

In my present school the head custodian/building engineer is a very hard working man who does his best to keep the building clean. He was hired thirty some years ago to shovel coal into a furnace. He worked hard and continued to be promoted. Now he is expected to operate a computerized climate control system in a block square building that has three stories and five wings. He has been sent to a couple of seminars on computers but does not seem to have any comprehension of programming or adjusting the programming of computers. About every three or four years Honeywell Controls is given a contract to get the system working correctly again.

Our head custodian has the most seniority, so he has his pick of schools and he likes this school. Lucky us! Our custodian is an outstanding example of either an American success story—success due to diligent hard work or the Peter Principle—take your pick. Unfortunately when he retires, we will get another head custodian just like him (see Farber's postulate #6; Le Chatelier's principle is the principle that operates most schools).

—

One of the problems at urban high schools is student abuse of the lavatories. (This is a problem at most schools.) This school is three stories high and was built with lavatories on *each* floor of *each* of its five wings and in the main corridor. (Don't be a lazy reader, do a little math) Of course any school child could have told the architects that it would be difficult to monitor all of these facilities. The school board, in its finite wisdom, chose to delete from its personnel budget all but a single hall monitor for each floor. This allowed the lavatories to be vandalized and/or be a source of trouble. The administration decided that the solution to the lavatory problem was to lock all but one or two of the lavatories. Since no one lavatory is large enough to handle the needs of almost three thousand students without running out of supplies, etc., there were many complaints about the lack of cleanliness and lack of basic supplies. The school's solution to this problem was to close lavatories when their odor became too strong for all but the bravest or most desperate of students and to open another lavatory as the day goes on.

To further relieve the problem of dirty lavatories, more changes were instituted. First, lavatories were locked during class change so that students are not late to class. Then teachers are not permitted to give students lavatory passes until ten minutes into the class period. Only one student was permitted to leave the class at a time. This policy was supposed to solve the problem.

Let's look at the situation realistically. A student is given a pass to the lavatory but has no idea where the open lavatories are at the moment. It is harder for a student to find the open lavatory than it is for the principal to find the daily floating craps game. The student is out of the class for at least fifteen minutes but often more than an half hour. There are about 30 students in a class which means that only about three students can use the rest room per period. There are seven periods in the school day. That means some students will not be able to get permission to use the rest room at all during the school day. Most will not be allowed to use it when they want to use it. Is it any wonder there is a smell of urine in fire towers and stair wells? But if we have any surprise bigwig visitors, we can show them a dozen clean, well-stocked lavatories, as soon as someone can find the key to unlock them.

—

There is always someone complaining about the standards of any school. Everyone wants the school to have higher standards but no one wants their child to be given a lower grade. This is analogous to the fact that everyone wants to get to heaven but no one wants to die. Naturally when administrators are faced with a no-win situation, it is turned over to the teachers to decide what and how to do it.

Teachers are the main part of the American educational system and therefore have forsaken any semblance of logical thinking in accordance with Farber's first postulate. Early in my teaching career I had my first experience with teachers trying to uphold academic standards.

This happened at the monthly junior-senior high school faculty meeting. The question to the faculty in attendance at this meeting was whether an A should be 90% or 91% and should passing be 60% or 61%?

The math oriented people argued that each grade range should have the number range and thus an A should be 91% to 100% which is ten numbers whereas there are eleven numbers that would result in a grade of A if 90% was an A. This position was supported by those teachers who wanted to raise the school's academic standards (as if 1% really would make a difference). They also thought that this would give us more prestige.

The traditionalists argued that 90% was the standard for years, and that since it worked, there was no need to change. What was more worrisome for both the liberals and conservatives was the lowest passing grade. Should it be 60% or 61%? Some wanted a policy that passing was above 60 while others wanted a policy that an F was any grade below 60%. Some worried about failure rates increasing and argued to make 60% the lowest passing grade. They said that the higher number would hurt our borderline students. Some teachers who wanted to make A grade begin at 91% now changed sides when discussing the lowest passing grade.

The discussion was rather confusing to me as a new teacher. It seemed to be going in circles. After listening to this for some time, I could not understand what all the fuss was about. I asked a simple question.

"I want you to tell me what a student should know for an A or *what it is* that the student should be able to do correctly 90 % or 91% of time to get an A?

I didn't think that this was a dumb question. Actually I thought it was a logical question. The other teachers looked at me as if I was speaking a foreign language. I thought that maybe they did not hear me or that I did not communicate my question correctly. I rephrased my question …

"Is there a body of knowledge in each subject area or a set of skills that constitute what a student could or should learn to have succeeded in the course?"

Now they looked at me like I was stupid. But I gave it one more try.

"If you say that a student got 95% of your course requirements or knowledge, tell me what is 100% of *the* knowledge or skills that a student could or should learn from the course?"

At this point they all just ignored me and went back to their original arguments which continued until the meeting time ran out. This discussion continued at the next meeting and was settled by a vote. I don't remember which way the vote went, I just remember that I didn't speak or vote at that second meeting.

A few years later the same faculty "raised" the standards of the school by voting that the lowest passing grade in any subject would be 70%. They did not ever say 70% *of what* the student had to be able to do or learn. By this time in my career, I knew better than to ask. The actual number of A's, B's, C's, D's, and F's did not change from one year to the next or from one standard to the next. (This is also an example of Farber's postulate #6; Le Chatelier is the guiding principle at all schools.) This is an indication to me that teachers or schools have no absolute standards but that students are really graded on a "curve" no matter what the official school "policy" states.

—

Another yard stick of the "success" of a school is the scores of its students on "standardized tests." Almost every school wants to say that its students score at or above their "grade level." Of course "grade level" is a mathematical average which means that about 1/2 of the students score above and 1/2 score *below* this mean.

What this means is that for every school district that has the majority of its students scoring at or above grade level, there must be another school district that has an equal number of students scoring at or below grade level. The school district that did not do well on the tests will soon stop giving the test. When this happens, the average scores will begin to increase. Therefore the scores that define "average" for each grade level will rise.

The trick used by many of the school districts is to develop their own "standardized test." This is an in-house test that compares the present students only to students from the previous year in the same district. The first year that the test is given, neither the teacher nor students know what to expect or exactly how to prepare for the test. Then the next year, the teachers know what to expect on the test and can better prepare the students for the test. Because of this, the district average is a bit higher the second year. Each successive year both the teachers and the students know more about the *district standardized testing program* and can increase the scores. This process will continue for a few years. When the scores no longer are increasing, it is time for the district to write or buy a "new standardized test." This makes it easier for a superintendent or school board to proclaim that the school system is doing well.

A really astute superintendent of public schools or headmaster of a private/charter school will eliminate all standardized testing in his/her domain. I remember one newly appointed individual who gave an opening speech to the faculty in which he proudly announced the goal of making our school "numero uno." He then went on to announce that our progressive programs would be not subjugated to the tyranny of standardized tests. Only someone who did not understand Farber's first postulate would be foolish enough to ask how we could be *number one* in education if our students were not going to be compared by standardized tests to students in other school districts.

—

In my state the department of education decided to give standardized reading and math tests to all students. They wanted these tests as an indicator of how well each district was doing as well as to determine the general level of accomplishment of students in this state.

The local school boards wanted no part of this program. The results of the tests would be made public, and some districts and schools would look bad. The teachers' organizations backed the local school boards in opposing this program.

The state solved the problem by paying any district an extra subsidy based on the number of the students that were *two or more grade levels below average*. It did not take the major school districts long to realize that this was a way to enhance their income. Only in education would we try to improve standards by giving schools extra money *only* if they were substandard. In simple terms, *the state rewarded failure*. This is neither logical nor intelligent. Thus it was a program that fit well in the educational scheme.

—

Our school, like many urban schools, has a problem with teenage pregnancy. While there is a lot of talk about ways to reduce the rate of teen pregnancy, the school spends more money on programs for teen mothers than on prevention programs. We have infant day care in the high school. On the surface this seems logical. The day care program will allow teen mothers to attend school regularly and graduate. But when teachers complained that teen mothers were putting their babies in the school day care and then cutting all their assigned classes several days each week, we were told that this was none of our business. Once again, logic does not apply to school programs.

There is even a program that gives a teen mother, who graduates from our high school, two years free tuition at the local community college. Teen fathers don't get the same break—yet.

—

There are those who will point to the private schools as better schools. Most private schools have an entrance standard. Public schools must accept any student who lives in the geographic boundaries of the school district.

The private school can expel students for misbehavior. The public schools can not. The public school finds it has fewer tools with which to discipline students every year. When a school can not effectively discipline and can not expel disruptive students, the education component of the school is in jeopardy.

The private school can expel or flunk students out of the school who do not progress according to the school's academic minimums. The public school must keep students until a certain age. In most districts, students are kept until age 21, and in some urban districts students may attend until age 25. In most public schools, students over age 21 may not be on varsity sports.

I taught in a private school that did not accept any student who did not have an IQ of 100 or more *and* was doing math and reading on or above grade level. This school then expelled the lowest 10% of the high school students each year. This school had a reputation for the excellence of the education that it provided to its students. This is just another example that logic does not apply to education. Any school that has acceptance standards that eliminate all but the best students and then proceeds to sort out and graduate only the best of the best students can be known as an excellent school.

Now the question is *are private schools providing a better education?"* The fact is that they accept only "better" students, retain only successful students and thus graduate a better, more able student. If you judge a school by its graduates, you can effectively argue that private schools are better schools. Private schools start with a selective and more affluent student body. Upon graduation, these students are far more likely to start off in higher paying jobs. Hopefully, you have determined that logically this does not answer the question since it does not say that the school has done a better job teaching or "educating" its students. This is a moot point since *logic does not apply in education.*

—

Colleges and universities can do the same thing. Any school that can limit admissions to only the better students and can *afford* to flunk out a percentage of these will be known as an excellent school. In the 1950s and 1960s when there was a shortage of college classroom space, most colleges maintained rather high academic standards. Those who attended college in these decades will often recall that their most difficult courses[4] were sophomore courses. Most of the students who flunked out did so in the first two years. Now the colleges have scheduled these courses as junior level courses. This keeps classrooms and dormitories filled for a longer time. As colleges and universities expanded they were forced by

---

4   Every department of a college or university has certain courses that are "screening" courses. These are used to maintain the department standards. Students who fail to pass these screening courses may change to another major or may drop out of college.

monetary considerations to accept and retain students that were performing at lower levels.

We have all heard about the "grade inflation" that has become the
norm in many schools. Professors who want to get tenure and maintain
their standard of living must not have a standard that results in students
avoiding their sections. In many colleges, students are not expected to
maintain a full course load. In these schools, it is almost normal to take five
years to complete a four year program. This works to the school's advantage
since the standard tuition buys a full course load that is then not used. The
school pockets the difference.

The academic standards of a college or university today depend more
on the recruiters than the professors. If the recruiters can attract better
students to the college then the college can have, or claim to have, higher
academic standards. The most important role of the professors is to publish
or do newsworthy research that helps the school's recruiters. I know of no
case where a professor was denied tenure for poor teaching. The college
does not even consider the teaching ability of the teachers in the hiring and
retention of its teachers. Students (and their parents) spend a great amount
of money to attend a college that has a good reputation. This is just one
more example of the fact that *logic and intelligence has no place in education,* even in higher education.

—

As the well-known prayer goes, "give us the strength to change that which
we can change and to endure that which can not be changed, and the wisdom to know the difference." Your job as a teacher is to increase knowledge
and enhance the mental abilities of your students, endure the inadequa-
cies of the educational system and, by acceptance of the first postulate, not
waste your limited time and energies trying to change the system. If you
choose to become a school principal or superintendent, then you can try
to change the system.

It is my hope that, after reading this book and reaching a better understanding of the educational system, you will enjoy teaching and not expend energy trying to change things outside of your classroom.

CHAPTER 2

Farber's Second Postulate

INDIANS (AND STUDENTS) NEVER ATTACK CRAZY PEOPLE

The beginning teacher is usually given this advice from an experienced colleague: "Get the students into the room, close the door, and handle your own problems. Don't send students to the department head, dean or principal for misbehavior." Follow this advice and if no one is killed or sued, you will get another contract next year. This may be a sad commentary on education but it is true!

So how do you control the kids without some help? Good question! There is no simple answer. Some people never figure it out and there is nothing that works *all* the time. Some things work for some people but not at all for other people. If you find a way that works all the time, call me *immediately*. We will make a fortune.

Do you remember the old cowboy and Indian movies where the Indians attack the wagon train? The situation is hopeless, and someone must escape to get help from the Cavalry. About this time someone starts walking out toward the Indians chanting or singing nursery rhymes and the Indians don't bother the "crazy" person. Students respond to "crazy" people in much the same way. Kids may act crazy, but they have a keen instinct for self-preservation. There is nothing they fear more than an adult that *is* as crazy as they act.

Being a science teacher has some built-in advantages. Students enter the classroom with the preconceived notion that scientists are a bit weird.

This is a result of TV and movies, (and who said kids aren't prejudiced?) I figured why fight it-just go with the flow. Anyhow, it is hard to dispel any prejudice and we teachers must save our energy to fight more important prejudices.

Teachers of other subjects use costumes, hand puppets and even imaginary friends to convince students that they are a little bit crazy.

I replaced the school clock with one that I had built to look like the classroom clock, but the numbers are going in reverse order from the normal clock. The hands also move in the opposite direction.[5] I never get completely through the first class period of the first day of the school year without someone raising their hand and asking "what's wrong with the clock?"

I patiently explain that there is nothing wrong with the clock and that this is a non-digital clock. I continue by explaining that the little hand points to the hour and the big hand points to the minute. Then I continue the lessons as if nothing is unusual about the clock. This of course upsets the students who insist that the clock is not right. I check the time on the clock against my watch and can not find anything wrong about the wall clock. It may take a while but finally some student will finally be able to clearly express the idea that hands on clocks usually rotate in the opposite direction. At this point I launch into a discussion about how clocks are based on sundials and that shadow on sundials rotate in different directions in the northern and southern hemispheres. I stress the need to look at things from different perspectives to more fully understand the world etc. I tell them that this is how most mechanical clocks would look if clocks had been first developed by someone living in the southern hemisphere.

The students begin to give each other those questioning looks that say "this guy is off the wall." This is the beginning of the development of an uneasy, wary class. This class will be more alert and begin to *think* about things that are going on in the classroom. It could be the beginning of

---

5   The reverse clock, also known as a barbershop clock, can be built from a kit from craft catalogues or found on the internet.

learning something about science.

Interestingly enough, the students quickly adapt to telling time on the reverse clock. We educators have been accused of graduating kids who can't read but no one ever said our graduates can't tell time—especially break time or quitting time. Sometime during the second semester I've been known to replace the reverse clock with a 24 hour clock. It's never dull or predictable with a crazy teacher.

—

Sometime during the first week of chemistry class I arrive in class wearing a black magician's cape. I tell the students that in a previous life I was an alchemist. (If they had doubts about my sanity, this ends all doubts) I explain that the goal of every alchemist was to change base metals into gold. I go on to explain that I don't make a big salary as a teacher so I make a little gold now and again to help make ends meet. Of course, if everyone could make gold it would not be worth much so I keep the secret to myself.

Then I proceed to change pennies into gold (actually the pennies have been brass plated). Naturally the students say that it can't be done or it is just a trick. I stick to my claim that I have made gold and dare them to "scientifically prove" that the pennies are not gold. The result is that they think the teacher is wacko but they begin using *scientific methods* to prove their teacher is trying to fool them. They actually go to the library and look up characteristics and properties of gold. They ask jewelers how to tell if something is "real" gold. It gets things going in the right direction from my point of view.

Sometimes the *right* direction is to go to the counselor to get a schedule change. It is often the students who are reputed to be the biggest classroom problems who are the first in line at the counselor's office to get out of my class. After seeing my antics they are not sure how I will respond to *their* antics. It is amazing how students can manipulate the system. If I, a teacher, wanted to transfer these students out of my class, it would be next to impossible. The students, on the other hand, seem to be able to work the system with amazing ease.

In biology class I often teach a period or two with a live mouse or rat in my lab coat pocket. Other times I have had a live snake over my shoulders or up my sleeve as the students entered the class. After this I usually don't have any trouble keeping their attention, with rare exceptions. (If an administrator or a parent questions my methods, I just tell them that this helps set a tone for the study of living things.)

—

Sometimes nothing will keep their attention. I taught in a boys' boarding school where the noon meal was the big meal of the day. It was an hour long dinner. It was hard to keep the class truly alert after this heavy meal. There was John in the front center of the class who seemed to fall asleep no matter what was happening in class. Now I am not one to permit such a thing. I started off by correcting John, then making loud noises to startle him awake and finally he was assigned after school detentions. Nothing normal seemed to alter his after dinner sleeping habit.

Since I was teaching both biology and chemistry, I had quite a few things at my disposal. I tried rubbing several foul smelling chemicals on his desk but John learned to sleep with his head back away from the desk. I put a live, five foot long king snake in his lap—the lazy snake went to sleep too. I powdered his hair white as he slept and when he awoke we told him that he had slept twenty years like Rip Van Winkle. I painted his face several times. Nothing succeeded in keeping John awake. It became a running joke in the school and the class couldn't wait to see what I would do next. Finally I brought in my daughter's baby doll and tucked it in sleeping John's arm and took pictures-blackmail pictures. A picture of a sixteen year old boy sleeping with a baby doll! A picture of John sleeping with a baby doll in the senior yearbook was a serious threat. It got the attention of all the adolescent boys in my classes, except John.

While I didn't succeed with John, my reputation grew. Once the students decide that you are crazy and thus unpredictable they treat you with respect. It does not matter what the students say about you as long as they say it with respect. Therefore it is important to set this tone of unpredictability early in the school year.

—

Classroom control and procedures are always up to the teacher. It is always best to start out on the strict side with clear rules and expectations. These are best written and posted in the room. The only thing that succeeds is to be *consistent and persistent* in your expectations. This may not seem logical after what I just said about being unpredictable (*logic does not apply in education*) but students will respond to your *predictable expectations,* especially if that is the only predictable thing about your class. Whatever works now at the beginning of the school year may not work later in the school year, so you must be ready to change your method but not your *expectations.* You must be persistent and try many methods to reach the same goals. What works for the teacher next door may not work for you.

When teachers come to me for help I usually give them examples of things other teachers are doing that are successful. These things may be as different as night and day. Teaching is an individual thing and each teacher must discover what will work for him or her.

Some teachers always have "pre-class" work on the board for the students to copy in the beginning of class period while the teacher takes attendance and does the administrative paper work. The students know that this will be erased in a few minutes so they must settle down and copy it. This gets students in their seats and quiets the class. Other teachers start the lesson immediately while others just muddle through.

There are teachers that give a daily grade for class deportment and others require the students to take daily notes which are graded weekly. Most teachers find this too much work.

While I may be lazier than most people, I'm not dumb. I have been known to give a quiz every day for the first month of school. Most students have never had such a demanding teacher. They quickly realize that it is impossible to find enough excuses to justify failing a simple five question quiz every day of the week. (Even excuses to a mother who is usually willing to believe anything in defense of her child will wear thin in this situation). Grading a hundred and twenty or more quizzes every evening sounds like lot of work but it is easier to work hard for one month and at the same time eliminate problems (or problem students) early, than it is to have problems that continue through the entire school year. The students, who are looking for a way to an easy grade usually, find their way to a counselor with a creative reason to transfer out of my class. Once the students realize that a teacher is willing to do something like this, they are more cooperative, especially when you run classes like a "normal" teacher. *Sane people never want to upset a crazy person, especially when the crazy person is behaving "normally."*

—

It is imperative that a teacher discover methods to deal with the administrative nuances (school rules and procedures) in a way that does not detract from education. Enforcing these things, writing passes, etc., can take so much time and effort that there is little left for actual teaching.

One of the "big" problems at one school was students wearing hats in class. The school had a policy that no student could have a hat on their head. One vice principal made this his primary mission in life. He "wrote up" four teachers, threatening them with the loss of their positions because he peeked through the window in the classroom door and saw students with hats.[6] Since caps are very popular this rule made life difficult for all

---

6   It didn't seem to occur to this vice principal that teachers should be concerned about what was in the students' heads rather than what was on them. Of course a hat is instantly visible while a bright thought is not.

teachers. In each of my classes I announced that I would take all the caps worn in class and nail them to the ceiling. Then I went down to the 'lost and found' department and collected about a dozen hats. Every day I would nail another one of these caps to the ceiling of my classroom. Each day, as each different class of students entered the room, I would ask if anyone wanted to contribute to my cap collection by wearing a cap. The problems of cap wearing ended in my room without any disruption of education. The vice principal in charge of hats came into my room, looked up at the ceiling, and never came in my room again that school year. It seems that even chiefs and vice principals leave crazy people alone.

Hall passes are another nuisance that take up much of a teacher's time. Standard procedure in most schools is that a teacher may excuse only one student from the room at a time *and* that student must have a "hall pass." Once a student leaves the room with a pass he/she can take their good old time, wander the halls and there seems no reasonable way the teacher can determine the truth as to why they were gone so long or exactly where they were as opposed to where they were supposed to be. Of course as soon as one student returns another student is in dire need of a hall pass to the restroom, etc. so the lesson in interrupted again and again. One year I had a group of ninth grade boys that had some sort of a hallway or lavatory fixation. Every one of them wanted a pass everyday as if it were some sort of a contest to see who could spend the most time out in the hall. I had to put a stop to this so I got a cement block and painted it gold (*a gold brick for the gold brickers*). I stenciled "HALL PASS" on both sides of it and that became the hall pass that the boys had to carry. Wandering the halls became less fun when they had to carry this heavy block of a hall pass.

Of course word got around about my hall pass. One day when I was talking with the headmaster at lunch he brought up the subject of my hall pass. He asked "What am I going to say to the mother of the boy who drops that block on his foot?"

I replied that if I were smart enough to handle that situation then I would be the headmaster. This was the end of the discussion about the gold brick hall pass. He never directed me to discontinue the use of the block as a hall pass. I guess that he was afraid of what I might do instead of this. Big chiefs respect (or avoid) crazy people too.[7]

Of course I am not the only crazy teacher around. One teacher used a toilet seat as a hall pass. Considering the condition of some of the urban school lavatories, I wonder if this toilet seat served a dual purpose.

—

Every day teachers are faced with students who come to class without the proper tools. This is not a new problem to education. I'm sure that students forgot their slates a hundred years ago and their burnt sticks which were used for writing two hundred years ago. The most common tool that students forget to bring to class today is a pen or pencil. A teacher can easily give out a box of pencils every day. This gets costly after a while so teachers devise ways of avoiding this. Some teachers sell pencils. This can be a problem. Some students end up "owing" the teacher money. Try collecting from a student!! This is usually trouble with a capital T.

Most teachers try to "lend" pencils to students but the students generally forget to return the pen or pencil. Soon this is almost as costly as giving out pencils. Someone suggested to me that I hold a "security" deposit when I lend a student a pen or pencil. I thought this was a good idea and I found that the students would offer me a watch, ring, or wallet to hold as security. I would put these in my desk drawer and then at the end of class I would return them when the student returned the pen. Well that is what was supposed to happen. More often than not the student would walk out with my pen and I would have a drawer full of watches and wallets at the end of the day which I had to find a way of securing until the students returned to claim them. I would often not be sure who gave me which ring

_____

7   This is also an example of Farber's fifth postulate: *It is better to give than receive—so give everyone a rough time.*

or watch by the next day or week when the student returned. I knew that this was trouble.

No one seemed to have a solution to this problem. It was a professional challenge that I couldn't resist trying to be the first to find a solution that would work one hundred percent of the time. And now I am going to let you in on the solution to this age old problem.[8] When a student comes to my class without a pen or pencil, I will provide one only if the student gives me one shoe as a security deposit. I have never had a student walk out of class wearing *only one* shoe and not remember that he or she needs to return a pencil or pen. *Do not* allow a student to give you both shoes as a security deposit. Believe me, there are students that will leave class and not notice that they are not wearing shoes. But I have never had a student get very far with one shoe on and one shoe off that did not notice something was not quite right.

I know that this solution sounds crazy, but crazy works in education.

—

Students bring all sorts of electronic devices to school today. These range from computer games to music players and phones. The school policy is that these things do not belong in school and that teachers are to "take" them. Some of these items are expensive and/or cherished by the kids. Following school policy can lead to big confrontations and problems. One can not expect to be backed by the administration for following administrative policy. *This would be too logical.* One can also expect to be reprimanded for not following policy. My solution to this problem is to take the batteries out of the devices. I get quite a collection of batteries early in the school year and the science department no longer needs to buy batteries for the electrical study units any more. By the second grade report period I no longer "see" any electronic devices in my classroom.

---

8   This may be my most important contribution to American education.

In every class there are students who lean back in their chairs and rock on two legs. Since ecology and conservation is part of the science curriculum, it is something I practice in the classroom. Conservation is not wasting your resources. In other words, a good conservation practice should be taking and using only what you actually need to do the job. I decided that *chair legs* should be conserved. I removed the front legs from one of the chairs to make a two legged chair for those students who did not want to or need to use all four legs of their chairs. A few students each year would demonstrate that giving them a four legged chair was a waste of chair legs. They would be assigned the two legged chair for a period or two. They would quickly decide that thousands of years of chair design that resulted in our standard four legged chair has merit. A history lesson in science class! What will happen next? They're not sure. This fact keeps them alert and paying attention thus learning more. And, oddly enough, they all started using all four legs of their chairs.

—

Many perspective teachers have their first real teaching experience as a substitute teacher. This is one of the more demanding situations in teaching. The students know that you don't know them by name and they do not know you or your reputation. They know that you will be here only for a short time, so none of the long term things like grades or behavior marks will be a consequence of anything that happens now.

I worked as a substitute for a short period of time. This occurred when my school had lengthy strike and I took substitute work in another district. Being an experienced teacher, I realized the need for an "instant" reputation. My solution to this problem was to wear a rear view mirror on my glasses. This can be purchased in bicycle shops. The first time I would write on the board, I would watch for a student who was doing something wrong. I would then verbally identify the offender and reprimand the student without turning around and looking at him or her. By the third period of the school day, word would get around the school that there was a crazy sub in science class who was wearing a rear view mirror and seemed very unpredictable. The students never attacked the crazy substitute teacher.

—

This keeping students uncertain is not something which I invented, rather it is something that schools have had in place for a very long time. It has been a part of the discipline systems in schools or rather a part of the student control system. It is kept better concealed today since it is not politically correct.

As beginning teacher I was concerned that there was not a set penalty for each rule violation or offense. I campaigned for a formal student code of conduct with levels of offenses and punishment according to the level. I wanted the school to be fair by treating all students alike. I was stopped by the administration and discipline committee. It was none of my business.

It is not my nature to accept such an answer. I compiled a list of students who had committed the same infraction and their punishments which ranged from none to rather severe.

Now I could not be completely ignored. I got a reply from the chair of the discipline committee. He said that my idea of a formal code of rules with levels of offenses and punishments was a foolish idea that could not help our school. He said that what I was proposing was just like a menu with a list of items and the price of each. (I thought that this was logical) He then went on to suggest that some students might find the prices acceptable or even a bargain! No, he insisted that each case must be decided on an individual bases and that the punishment, if any, would be whatever the committee decided suited the situation.

I thought that this man's position was just plain crazy. Later I realized that the objective was to have the students follow the rules of the school and that the fear of the unknown is a greater incentive than knowing the punishment. In other words, crazy works!

Today most schools are more structured with codified rules and possible punishments spelled out for students and parents. The minor infractions are still best handled by the teacher. Major offenses are handled by deans or administrators. However what is a major offense to a teacher may be considered a minor offense to someone else or visa-a-versa. Let me give you an example from my own recent experience.

Daryl was a "new admit" part way through the year to my last period chemistry class. He was just eighteen and had just been released from a local institution having served time for mugging. He was a good student for a couple of months, then he began cutting class and becoming disruptive when in class. Talking with him helped a little and writing cut slips (paperwork recording class cuts and threatening action) only made problems worse. One day he showed up to class quite drunk and I finally had to get help from two school security people to remove him from my class. He was back in school the next day. Drunkenness cannot be recorded or punished unless medical tests give proof. This is a hassle for the school and costs money—which is always in short supply. The classroom disruption is the teacher's problem, in other words not serious. Drug testing may infringe on the student's rights! In short, the school system will do nothing. Daryl was back in my class the very next day.

Several weeks later Daryl suddenly disappeared from school and no one seemed to know where he was or why he was not in school. Frankly, most of the staff counted his absence as a small blessing. Then I met him on the street near the school and asked him why he was not attending school.

"Well, Mr. Farber, " he began, "that school was most unfair to me. It's not fair at all. They threw me out. I didn't do nothin' and they expelled me."

"What happened sounds like it was unfair? Maybe I can help you." I replied.

"You know that it's not my style to take stuff from people," he said. "You see, I was just fooling 'round in the hallway and this old fart comes up to me and started on me. Like, I just told him where he could put it. That's all I did. How was I supposed to know that he was the principal? You people should wear some kind of signs."

Daryl had been expelled for something that he did regularly to students and teachers but *we* had no recourse but to take his abuses. He never got back in school.

Is there a moral to this story? No- not that I can figure out. It's just that the system is still crazy under the veneer that is presented in the student handbooks. It is like military justice. It may be called justice but it is meant to instill fear. Man may be the most feared (or fearsome) creature on the Earth but he is still afraid of the dark (read 'unknown').

Students are unnerved by the unknown and grope for something that they can depend on or for some sort of predictability. This is how you can now become a successful teacher. You *must be consistent and persistent in your objectives*. Your students will detect this and cling to these like a shipwrecked sailor to a life ring. They will reach for the security of meeting your course objectives since these are the only things that they can count on in your class.

Persistence does not mean that you approach an objective the same way each time. You can attack the objective from exactly opposite directions from day to day , week to week , lesson to lesson or chapter to chapter but if you are *consistent* in your expectations of student outcomes, your students will live up (or down) to your expectations. I mention *down* because other teachers will often tell you that certain classes or students can not be expected to perform at higher levels of performance or behavior. Don't believe them! It just means that they have not found a way to reach these levels. You can usually get students to learn and behave at any reasonable level. You must set objectives for your students and be persistent. There is study after study in education that provides evidence that student achievement can be altered by the teacher's expectation. This is often a self-fulfilling prophecy that can be controlled by faculty room gossip about the abilities of students. If you don't fall into the trap of believing this, then your students can and will achieve above the expectations of other staff members. (This may not make you popular with certain other teachers who are never wrong).

—

Being a bit crazy allows one to approach and solve many of the everyday school problems. For instance, fights can erupt, without warning, in the hallway as classes are changing. The usual procedure is for the teacher to try to prevent and/or break up the fight. Many teachers try to get between the students to keep them apart, but there have been several teachers hurt doing this. Teachers try to talk to the students to try to resolve their disagreements in a more civilized manner. This usually results in the opponents screaming and shouting their positions which attracts an even larger group of spectators and, unless the teacher gets help, can result in a small riot.

I was in the hallway once, when a fight started between two students. I pushed my way through the crowd and when I got to the combatants, they were still in the cursing and shoving stage of the fight. I immediately took out my pocket camera to get some good pictures. This is really disturbing to students since they want to be properly posed for photographs that may be circulated. (Of course, today everyone has a phone that takes pictures and then they show up on the internet). Then I demanded a dollar fee from all those spectators in the front rows. I made it clear that there was not going to be any *free* entertainment in my area of the hallway. At this point the combatants were getting confused as to why they were going to fight and who was, *really* going, to come out ahead in this fight. It began to look like I had more to gain than either of the students since they would be suspended when it was over and I would have a pocket full of money. At this point they started with "I'll see you after school in the parking lot" routine. I told them that this was a better idea and that if they could have their fight below the chem lab windows I could get a very good price for my "sky box" window seats. "Let's get the time set up so that I can maximize the ticket sales."

At this point they decided that they really didn't want to fight since the teacher was going to promote the fight and profit from it.

We have had many meetings and in service days devoted to preventing fights in the school because this is a growing problem in today's schools. The fact is that school is a good place to have a fight since usually no one gets seriously injured. The students count on the fact that a teacher will break up the fight after just a few punches are thrown. Unfortunately many teachers are injured as they attempt to stop the fight. When I am forced to attend these meetings I always suggest that the school set up a boxing ring and let the students fight it out after school. In my school we could have ten or fifteen fights on the card each week. Using oversize gloves and good officials no one would get hurt and we could benefit. With the right promotion we could sell out every seat in the gym each week and use the money to buy new science equipment and computers.[9] We could make it a school rule that students *must* fight at least five rounds after school instead of having them sit after school in a detention hall. This would probably reduce the number of fights in our school faster than a dozen anti-violence programs.

Usually after I make this perfectly logical proposal the moderators of the meeting are perfectly happy to let me sit in the back of the room and grade papers, prepare lesson plans, read a book or make good use of my time rather than wasting it in meetings that accomplish nothing.

—

A teacher who is not afraid of having the reputation of being a bit crazy can make the class more fun for the students. The class is more exciting and the students learn more. You never know what students will really remember.

In an effort to get a tenth grade biology class to think about evolution and how theories are developed by man, I announced that the next day we would have a guest speaker who would give a counter theory to the

---

9   Got to take care of my area of interest first-otherwise the money would disappear into the athletic department which already gets more money than all the academic departments combined. This follows Farber's first postulate since the *stated* primary objective of the school is to teach the students to use their minds.

accepted theory of evolution. The class assumed that the speaker would be presenting a creationist point of view.

The next day the students entered the room and took their seats in anticipation of my arrival with the guest speaker. At this point I entered the room in a gorilla suit and proceeded to present evolution from the point of view of a gorilla. Using charts and diagrams, I showed that man came before the great apes and was actually a lower, more primitive form of life. I took the point of view that man was handicapped by the lack of good instinctive behavior and therefore was a species that was in the process of destroying itself. I pointed out that the great apes do not beat their mates or children. Rape and murder are unheard of in the more civilized society of the apes, I told them. I ended the period long lecture emphasizing that although man may have developed better tools than apes, he does not have refined instincts to know how to best use them because mankind is nowhere near being civilized when compared to the apes.

About a dozen years later, I was in a shopping mall when a man approached me. He addressed me by name and told me that he was a former student of mine. He was now a lawyer. He said of all the things that he experienced in high school, what he remembered the most was the lecture by the gorilla.

We never know what we have actually taught our students. Thirty students in the classroom can have thirty different interpretations of the meaning of the lesson. We can expend much effort trying to teach serious science and some fun or unusual event will be what is actually remembered. My students are more likely to remember science demonstrations that didn't work than those that did.

Any teacher can use a costume to become a historical character, author or celebrity for their class. This character can be used to express alternative or unorthodox ideas. It can result in getting students to think and may lead to some interesting discussions.

Another possibility today is to use the internet and translation programs to see textbooks used in other countries. Imagine presenting the War of

1812 from a British textbook or the World Wars from a German textbook.

People who think outside of the box are often thought of as crazy. When they are successful, they are called geniuses. Either moniker will work for a teacher.

—

Each year in biology class the students are given the opportunity to dissect a variety of invertebrate animals and of course the infamous frog. Sometimes live frogs are used for experiments and vivisection. In my classes I added a new twist to all of this—cooking. I was usually able to buy clams, oysters, octopus, and snails at the local seafood market. If students had used live frogs, I would save the legs otherwise I would also buy frog legs. I would also buy some snails, mussels or clams, octopus and any other exotic delicacy available. I would then spend one day cooking all of these things for the students to sample. I told them that they needed to learn to cook as a life survival skill. I had to explain that not everything comes ready to cook in a microwave oven. I turned the lesson in to a regular gourmet cooking class. At first they would be reluctant to sample these unusual foods but after a couple of students tried and liked the samples, they would all get in the spirit to sample. Usually by the middle of the day, I would have a crowd of students from other classes hanging around outside of my class trying to get samples of the fun food.

This type of a lesson kept my students guessing about what I would do next.[10] Since they were never sure what this crazy teacher was going to do, they were more likely to be present in class and pay attention.

_____

10 This was to include cooking questions on the next test. I do not believe in "wasting time" or doing things to "entertain" students. Every lesson is to be educational, and part of the teacher's job is to determine what the students learned from the lesson.

—

In my ninth grade physical science classes Newton's laws of motion were a major part of the curriculum. The third law is "for every action there is an equal and opposite reaction." The best way to show this is by using rockets. A rocket with twice the engine force will travel twice the distance when launched horizontally from an elevated platform. The windows of my classroom were 52 feet above the ground and made an ideal launching site. The school parking lot was just beyond the window, followed by a road, then the soccer field and beyond that was a baseball field. Model rockets were shot horizontally out the window of my classroom for several weeks every year. Students were sent out to the fields to mark the locations of the various rocket impacts and to measure the distance the rockets traveled. Even the lowest powered rocket engine propelled the rockets well past the parking lot and road. Thus there was not a problem, at least from my point of view, with shooting rockets across the parking lot. Actually the staff seemed to get accustomed to rockets passing over their heads. Maybe they were just resigned to the situation since no sane person would lead an attack on such a crazy person.

Of course the rockets were not the only things that came out of my windows. When I wanted the students to measure the acceleration of a falling object, we dropped bricks out of the windows. We attached a narrow strip of paper to the brick and had a device that would put a mark on the paper at regular intervals many times a second. By measuring the distance between the marks, we could determine the rate the brick traveled for each time interval. Comparing these travel rates gave us the actual acceleration rate of the brick as it fell to ground below the classroom window. This was good way to learn science but it may seem crazy to those who do not know what we were trying to demonstrate.

When I wanted to demonstrate maximum force of a siphon, I used 32 feet of garden hose which I ran out of the classroom window. The hose would be attached to a gallon or larger can and both would be completely filled with water. Then the can would be inverted and the end of the hose dropped out of the window. I usually had a student holding the can. The water would drain quickly and completely from the can and the pressure of the atmosphere would crush the can. It was a great demonstration of atmospheric pressure but not well understood by those in the parking lot watching water draining from the hose extending from the window.

I also had a window with a demonstration bee hive in it. It was glass on two sides with a tube that went out through one of the classroom windows. In warm weather, there would be between 15,000 to 30,000 bees buzzing in and out of that hive. Bees have great ability when it comes to navigation. They almost never went to another other window and I could teach with the other windows open without any bees flying into the classroom. The students never got bored watching those bees and probably learned more about insects from the bees that they could have every learned from me.

All of these activities had sound educational goals behind them but seemed a bit crazy to those who did not take time to inquire about reasons for the activities. I adopted the attitude that my job was to educate my students and not the school staff. It is also true that if the faculty actually understood the educational value of these experiments, they would not think of me as crazy. My reputation of being unpredictable could be helpful. I avoided many committees' assignments and their boring meetings.

—

Sometimes craziness has some unexpected consequences. One time I was assigned to a new school at the end of January. Naturally I was given some classes that other teachers didn't care to try to teach. One of these was a ninth grade physical science class of 34 students, all of whom had flunked ninth grade science at least once before. This was the fourth go round for one lad. The grades from the previous teacher showed *only four* students with a passing grade for the first half of the present school year. The other 30 students had failed this class for the first half of the year.

I expressed my dismay at trying to teach this large uncooperative group. I was told not to worry about this class since they would stop coming to school as soon as the weather improved. It was believed that the only reason they were in school was because they were too dumb to find another warm place to hang out during the day.

I decided to do some demonstrations that might get them interested in learning science. One of these I call "catching the bullet."

The famous magician Houdini did a trick on stage where he stood behind a fine silk screen while an assistant shot a .32 caliber rifle at him. The screen would stop the bullet. The physics behind this is not difficult. The total force of the bullet is equal to the force that the rifle presses against the shoulder of the person shooting it however all the force of the bullet is concentrated in a small area. This is the reason that a bullet can punch a small hole in a solid object. The force of the rifle butt, which is equal to the force of the bullet, is spread over a much larger area. The silk screen reverses the process. It offers very little resistance to the bullet and wraps around the bullet. As the amount of silk carried by the bullet increases, it acts like a parachute on the bullet.

I found that I could do the same thing in the classroom using a pair of my wife's old panty hose and a 22 caliber air rifle. I demonstrated the power of the air rifle by shooting a few holes into some lumber and blocks. Then the panty hose were hung over a glass rod and I stood a foot or two behind it but off to one side. The science lab assistant, who is a good shot, then fired the rifle at the panty hose. As the bullet and the panty hose (acting as a parachute) flew off the rod, I grabbed the hose parachute and thus the bullet.

This was something I had done many times before but these lower achieving students who did not know me yet were quite impressed. (After 9-11 this was eliminated from my repertoire of science demonstrations.)

Warm weather came, and the students still came to class. Easter came and went and I still had a full class. The number of students with passing grades increased but still more than half failed the year. The failing students didn't want to work or learn science but it was entertaining. Success in teaching is open to many interpretations.

—

If there is anything that I really don't like, it is committees. I try never to serve on a committee that has more than 3 members. Committees are often formed to deal with problems that have no absolute solutions. However it relieves administrators of responsibility when things go wrong.

Because I was the teacher union rep of my building. I was required to be on the security committee. I did not volunteer. This was post 9/11. We had an airport security system in place. Each student had to walk through a metal scanner and their book bag was x-rayed. We had 2300 students and two scanners and x-ray machines. The students packed a long hallway every morning waiting their turn to go through the scanner.

Our written procedure was that if a student had a weapon, staff members were to call the school office. They were not allowed to call 911.[11] The secretary in the office would phone the police precinct so the call would not go out on the police radio where news people might be listening. We were assured that the police would arrive quickly.

The committee first spent time reviewing the present approved policy. Then we went around the room for comments and suggestions. Everyone on a committee feels that they must contribute something, which is why meetings can go on and on.

When I had enough of the polite cooperative discussion of the approved policy, I decided to rock the boat. I told them that they must be on drugs to believe that this would be an effective system of dealing with

---

11 Politicians who run the schools want to control negative publicity. See Farber's ninth postulate.

a student with a gun. I told them that the student would run out of bullets in our crowded hallways, especially the crowded area where students were waiting to be scanned, before the police arrived. The solution I suggested was to have a "school marshal" system modeled after the air marshal system of the airlines. The school could secretly pick a few staff members and send them to the same training as the air marshals. They could be secretaries, custodians, teachers or administrators.

Of course, they all looked me like I was crazy. They did not have a rebuttal to my suggestion. They solved the problem by ending the meeting. Then I was removed from the committee. I don't think that I was ever forced to be on a committee again in that school.

—

For many years I taught in a private boarding school. In addition to my teaching duties, I was responsible for one of the dormitories. Having the high school age students for 24 hours a day can create situations and problems that most teachers only have nightmares about. Students go into their rooms behind closed doors and all sort of strange things can take place. In college the students are legally adults and can be held responsible, but in the case of younger students, the adult in charge is held responsible.

The challenge of controlling a dormitory full of young, active, inventive minds requires a truly crazy person.

When I found that a student could not be trusted behind the closed door of his room, I solved the problem by removing the door to his room. You can just imagine the surprise and shock of the student when he came back to the dorm and found his door missing. Naturally he came running to tell me of the situation. I told him that I had taken the door to his room and had it in safe keeping until he demonstrated that he could be trusted behind it. He was sure that I was crazy and went to the next level of authority. Since that person already was sure I was nuts, he told the students that he was not going to get involved in the situation and that the student would have to make their peace with me.

If you can remember what it was like living in a dormitory and then think what it would be like to not be able to close your door to the noise of the hallway or the constant stream of visitors, you can then visualize how this door removal affected the students. They were really miserable without a door. Their behavior changed rapidly.

There were times that I was in possession of many as a half dozen doors but soon the students realized that it was better not to give me reason not to trust them. Then there would be several months or even a whole semester would go by without the need for me to remove a single door. This was because they were sure that I was crazy enough to do it.

There were other times when students would not keep their rooms clean. After repeated requests to clean up the room, I would declare the room unfit for human habitation. At this point I removed the student's bed, books, and basic clothes from the room, changed the lock on the door, and the student would reside in a part of one of the "public" rooms of the dormitory. We had rooms for TV, games, etc. Other students would let the student "crash "in their room. This usually lasted only a night or two. I only had to do this a couple of times and word got around. When I told a student to clean a room, I usually did not have to ask more than twice.

—

Experienced teachers will often state that they have heard every excuse. I am not sure that I have heard them all, but I kept a list. I told my students that I did not want to waste my time listening to their excuses for being late to class or for not having their homework. I posted the list of excuses that I had heard over the years on the wall outside of my classroom. I told them just to give me the number of their excuse so as not to waste my time. I further stated that I wasn't excusing them anyway.

This would save them time also.

For those of you who are just beginning your career in education, I will give you the list. There are many new excuses now with the greater use of computers. You will need to add these to the list.

Excuses for Being Late to Class

1. Breakfast is the most important meal of the day so I stopped to have breakfast.
2. I was coming from the basement.
3. The seniors were using me for a football.
4. There was a long line at the metal detectors.
5. The metals detectors kept beeping when I when through so they searched my book bag, purse, pockets, etc.
6. I went to the nurse.
7. I had a long test in the class before this one.
8. I fell asleep in class and no one woke me at the end of the period.
9. I twisted my ankle last night and now have to walk slowly.
10. I was in the lavatory.
11. I hadn't finished copying my friend's homework.
12. My teacher kept me after class but didn't write a note.
13. I lent my friend my biology book and had to wait until she returned it.
14. There was not any paper in the lavatory.
15. It was too noisy to hear the bells.
16. I was walking my friend to the nurse.
17. I was called to the office.
18. I was in the counselor's office.
19. There was a fire in the basement and I went to see if I could help.
20. I fell on the stairs.
21. I spent too much time looking for my homework.

22. Something got stuck in a tree and I was the only one who could get it.
23. There was a line at the lavatory after lunch.
24. I have a fear of insects and there was this huge bug in the stair well.
25. I was running to class and knocked myself unconscious by running into the fire extinguisher hanging in the hall.
26. The elevator go stuck.
27. The nurse was not in her office.
28. I was waiting for my friend to walk me to class.
29. I forgot my notebook and had to go to my locker to get it.
30. Some big kids stuffed me into a locker.
31. A girl in a wheelchair ran over my foot.
32. The secret service would not let me cross the street. (This only works when the President is speaking next door at LaSalle University.)
33. I got caught in a time warp.
34. There was a long line at the ice cream truck.
35. I spilled a drink and had to clean it up.
36. I could not get past the crowd in the hallway.
37. I witnessed a crime and was telling my story to an officer.
38. I was in the lunchroom thinking of whether I should cut or not. After a couple of minutes I decided to come to your class because it is so-o-o-o exciting.
39. I was studying.
40. A pigeon dropping hit my head and I had to clean it.
41. I was running so fast to your class that I missed the room.
42. I couldn't find the fifth floor pool.
43. I got wet in the rain.
44. My favorite lavatory is being repaired.
45. The lunchroom could not change a twenty so I had to wait until almost the end of lunch to get my food.

46. While I was having my lunch on the lawn outside, a rabid animal came toward me and I had to run really fast and far to get away from it.
47. The nurse couldn't find anything wrong with me.
48. I got an electrical shock when I tried to unplug the snack machine.
49. I was reading the grades you posted in the hallway and went into shock.
50. I was on the phone with my Mom because my dog is sick.
51. I got hit on by a cute guy.
52. I got sick eating the cafeteria food.
53. I got lost on the way to class.
54. I had to wait for my mother to bring my homework from home.
55. Someone broke into my locker.
56. I fainted in the hallway.
57. I was abducted by aliens.
58. I said hello to the principal and then he started talking to me.
59. My locker fell over.
60. I was wrongly accused for being the infamous cupcake thief.
61. I had to wait for school security to open my locker.
62. I got lost in the sub-basement tunnel of the school.
63. I had to walk my friend on crutches to class.
64. The lunch lady wouldn't take any money over $1.00 to buy a pretzel so I had to wait for change.
65. I jabbed myself with a pencil and had to get a Band-Aid.
66. I had to wait in line to get something to eat.
67. I slipped in a puddle in the hall. Then I cleaned it up so no one else would get hurt.
68. I was waiting for my friend to finish copying my homework.
69. I broke a nail.
70. I didn't have anyone to walk me to class.
71. I thought there was a fire drill.

72. I have short legs.
73. I forgot what schedule we are on today.
74. I had to check the weather.
75. I lost an earring.
76. All the school clocks show a different time.
77. I got my hand caught in a vending machine.
78. I can't walk fast with my pants low.
79. I had to explain to my last teacher why I was late for her class.
80. Late? Everyone else was early.
81. It's a genetic problem.
82. I got glue on my shoes.
83. I'm a senior.
84. You can call (teacher, counselor, nurse, etc.).
85. This is the fourth floor.
86. I was on my cell phone.
87. I was being interviewed by the newspaper.
88. I was waiting for my homework to print out.
89. I had to find my friend who had my homework.
90. Everyone liked my new hair (color, style, cut, etc.).

Excuses for Not Turning In the Homework

1. I lost the assignment.
2. My computer crashed.
3. It got wet in the rain on the way to school.
4. My friend wasn't in school today, so I couldn't copy it.
5. I lost my book bag.
6. My religion doesn't permit me to do homework about evolution or Darwin.
7. My printer ran out of ink.
8. I dropped it on the way to school and it blew into a sewer.
9. My little brother used it to make a paper mache mask.

10. I thought today was Sunday.
11. I was too upset. My parents told me Santa Claus isn't real.
12. I was late to class and didn't have time to go to my locker.
13. It was raining. I couldn't carry my umbrella and homework both.
14. My dog was missing and I spent the whole night searching for it.
15. I lost a contact and could not read.
16. I had to study for an English test. (You lose all brownie points with this one.)
17. I was held hostage at the 7-11 last night.
18. I left it on the bus.
19. I put it down to tie my shoes and it blew away.
20. I was mugged on the way to school and they took my book bag.
21. My friend is still copying it.
22. My sister and I had a fight and she tore up my homework.
23. My pet snake escaped and my mother did not allow me to do anything, including homework, until I found the snake.
24. I put it in the book that I forgot to bring to school today.
25. My printer ran out of paper.
26. My brother played a trick on me. He switched pens. I did all my homework with a disappearing ink pen.
27. My house caught fire last night.
28. I didn't have enough time to do it during English class.
29. My brother broke his arm last night and I spent most of the evening in the emergency room.
30. It was on the table and someone opened the window and it blew out.
31. My sister ate it.
32. I thought that I did the homework but then realized it was just a dream.
33. My cat peed on it.
34. My Mom made me take my sister to the park. While I was pushing her on the swing, some little kids with muddy shoes

walked on my homework.

35. I was going to fax it to a friend but put it in the shredder by mistake.

36. My friend took my homework and turned it in with his name on it.

37. The page with the homework questions has been ripped out of my textbook.

38. I left it in my other bag.

39. I was sick last night and couldn't do homework, but I got better and didn't want to miss school today.

40. I was doing it and my mother's boyfriend put a cigarette on it and it caught fire.

41. I dropped all of my stuff in the hall and someone with gum on their shoe stepped on my homework. It stuck to their shoe and they walked away before I could pick up all my stuff.

42. I went to the bathroom and there was no paper.

43. I left my stuff near a trash can and someone mistook it for trash and put it in the can.

44. I don't have my homework because my mother cleaned my room.

45. I didn't do my homework because I had to catch my gecko.

46. My dog had puppies.

47. I was in the hospital last night for severe hypochondria.

48. I was doing it at lunch and someone spilled on it.

49. I spent the evening celebrating passing your test yesterday.

50. I was checking out books from the public library for my extra credit science project.

51. I washed my book bag and forgot that the homework was in the bag.

52. I left the homework at my Dad's house. Mom would not get it since they are not speaking.

53. I had tickets to a Backstreet Boys concert.

54. The lunch period is too short to eat my lunch *and* do my homework.
55. Somebody broke into my locker and took my stuff.
56. The power was out in my neighborhood.
57. I was doing the homework in the lavatory and it got messed up.
58. I ran out of pens and pencils.
59. I locked my keys and homework in my car.
60. I did such a good job on my homework that I would make everyone look bad if I turned it in.
61. I left my books and homework on top of the car and then drove to school. It probably fell off along the way.
62. I broke up with my girlfriend and don't have anyone to do my homework.
63. My parents accidentally sent it in with their census forms.
64. My little brother made a paper football out of it.
65. I fell out of a tree yesterday and had temporary amnesia.
66. My computer crashed.
67. I was playing dominos and slammed the domino down so hard that my fingers swelled up so I couldn't do the homework.
68. The washing machine overflowed and the bleach destroyed my homework.
69. The acid rain on the way to school dissolved my homework.
70. I lost my list of assignments.
71. My shrink said that homework stresses me too much.
72. The police searched me this morning. The homework was missing when they returned my book bag.
73. It is locked in my friend's locker.
74. My friend was hung over and threw up on it.
75. It's not my fault. My last period teacher took it because I was doing it in her class.
76. I lost my textbook.
77. I was not allowed out of my room last night and my book was in

the kitchen.

78. My eraser put so many holes in it that it is destroyed.
79. My mother had a baby last night.
80. My dog died.
81. I have a "trigger" thumb that hurts if I use it too much.
82. My mother didn't get it done last night.
83. I got writer's block.
84. All of my loose-leaf paper got wet.
85. My mother made me clean up my room and by the time I got finished it was bed time.
86. My homework is so good that people keep stealing it.
87. When I finished my art project, I suddenly realized that I painted over my homework.
88. I did it in my native language and didn't have time to write a translation for you.
89. Glue got spilled in my book bag and all of my papers are stuck together.
90. My Dad took it to work to correct it and forgot to bring it home.
91. What homework?
92. My house was robbed yesterday. Everything was tossed and I could not find my homework in the mess.
93. I left it on the train platform.
94. It is in my other pants.
95. My parents took everything off of my bedroom floor and put down a new rug.
96. I couldn't find it on the web.
97. Our furnace went out and I had to burn it to keep warm.
98. The reason is none of your business.
99. I will not need to know this in the future.
100. There was a good program on TV last night.
101. My paper is evolving and becoming better, so I had to leave it alone for a while.

102. My friend sent the homework to the wrong email address.

103. I brought the wrong disk/CD/flash drive to school today.

104. When I sat down my disk/CD/flash drive was broken.

105. My laptop was stolen.

106. Didn't you get my email?

107. Anything as good as my work is worth waiting for …

108. I e-mailed it to myself at the wrong address.

109. My computer used a word processing program that the school's computers can't print.

110. My mother put it into my little brother's book bag.

111. It's in my computer but I can't find it.

112. It's on my mother's laptop and she was away with her boyfriend that my father doesn't know about.

113. The (library or Mr./Ms _____) won't let me print it on their printer.

114. We had an assembly this morning instead of advisory period.

This list[12] became well known to the students. Students would go out of their way to check the list for a good excuse to use with other teachers. It challenged students to do more thinking and be more creative. Crazy can cause creativity.

—

I'm sure that you have heard many adults exclaim that "these kids are driving me crazy." Kids will do things just to get attention or to annoy an adult. If they succeed with their crazy antics, they will continue doing such things at every opportunity. When the antics don't get the desired response, the kids discontinue them. When the teacher is prone to doing things which

---

12   While anyone is free to use my list of excuses, it will be more fun to compile a list unique to your school and students.

seem as outrageous as the kids' antics, it is threatening to the kids. They may even behave more like adults. As the old song goes, *"Ain't it great to be crazy?"* For a teacher it can mean survival. It is also a lot of fun. It helps you to learn not to take yourself, students or school systems too seriously.

CHAPTER 3

Farber's Third Postulate

NECESSITY MAY BE THE MOTHER OF ALL INVENTION, BUT LAZINESS IS CERTAINLY THE FATHER

By law in most states, children are required to attend school until the age of seventeen, and by law parents are required to send their children to public school unless they can afford private school.

The law does not require children to learn, do homework, be attentive or even behave in class.

The law does not require parents to help their children with homework, provide a place or time for children to read or study or to support the school program or teacher in any way.

Given this situation, there are a number of children who arrive everyday with the attitude "I'm here against my will and I defy you to teach me anything or to make me do anything." This often has tacit support from home. Many parents look upon the school as a day care center.

The school system expects the teacher to "motivate" the students to work and/or learn. The fact that work and learning are not the same thing is lost on many people. How to motivate students is up to the teacher. There are no simple answers to this dilemma and nothing will work all of the time.

The people who tell you just to make the subject interesting have never spent much time with teenagers. Sex, sports, current music and fashion are subjects of teenage interest. Everything else is boring. Chances are that you are not assigned to teach any of the things that interests teenagers.

It is possible to make a presentation exciting and/or fun. People point to the educational TV as an example of how you can improve your classroom. Given the time and tens of thousands of dollars that goes into a half hour TV show, it should be a good presentation. You will not be given either the time or the money to prepare your daily lessons on a par with a TV show. You may be teaching three different subjects that require three entirely different preparations each day. *You can not compete with TV*. You can probably not convince educational critics of this either.

The traditional methods of teaching are still used by the majority of the teachers because they are efficient and cheap. This is the *chalk & talk* method. The norm in most classrooms is that the teacher presents the material using the blackboard (It's stilled called this even though it is green) and then assigns some written exercises on the subject. Modern teachers have often replaced the board with an overhead projector and now power point projectors. Administrators usually accept this as 'good' teaching. Most parents remember this as how schools were back in the "good old days" when they got their education. For some teachers it solves their discipline problems. They bore students into submission.

Don't you remember that teacher who ordered every free or cheap movie and did nothing but show movies most of the time? This was known among teachers as the *celluloid curriculum*. It is not that movies are not useful from time to time, but they are not a substitute for real teaching. The steady diet of celluloid film allowed lazy people to collect a teaching salary for operating a film strip or movie projector.

Then we had magnetic video tape and the *magnetic curriculum* has come of age. The small screen sits in front of the classroom and the students get a steady diet of public television shows, Disney, and National geographic specials. The actual effectiveness of the small screen is not as satisfactory as the larger movie screen since the TV screen can't be seen well by all members of a class. However this mode is much easier and cheaper for the teacher and the school district. Students today seem to instantly get glassy eyed when a TV is turned on in front of them. Effective use of

TV means that the teacher integrates it with other modes of learning and interrupts the tape to allow students to take notes and to point out the more relevant parts of the presentation. This often means that the teacher must *edit* the tape to cut out all the fill that is often placed in programs to "stretch" to the time allotment of the program. In other cases it means that the commercials are eliminated. Most of this is in violation of some copyright law or another but no one seems to care as long as the students are contained in the classroom.

Now if the school is more affluent, there are computers, power point projectors and white/smart boards. This is the latest and most modern version and is known as the *laser curriculum*. This allows the big screen effect of the old *celluloid curriculum*. The less prepared teacher can couple the projector to his/her computer and surf the web as the class watches. Some teachers' lesson plans consist of a list of web sites that they think will be of interest to or will entertain students. In my present school, the wireless network went down one day. As the teachers' union officer, I started getting calls from teachers who didn't know what they were going to do since they "could not teach without the internet connection." I suggested that they try a marvelous teaching invention-chalk. (I'm not a union officer any more.)

While many school boards have been convinced that money spent on computers and computer software is an investment that will better prepare students for the workplace of today, computers can be used (or misused) by the schools. Many cheap software packages are not much better than a film strip but since the student must interact with the machine they don't fall (usually) asleep. There are the better interactive learning packages that work much like other computer games. Computers are a tool like the pocket calculator, slide rule, dictionary or thesaurus that allows the students to get information and helps them with writing and calculations. With wireless connections and students using laptops loaded with who knows what, it is difficult to direct and control what the students are actually doing.

These things all have their place but they will quickly become "boring" if used too much. "BORING" is the most common student description of school. If I blew the windows out of the chem lab on Monday and did it again Tuesday, on Wednesday the students would come into class and ask with a yawn, if I was going to do another *boring* explosion today. Using a variety of presentation methods is usually best for most classes.

Learning for the sake of learning or for the love of knowledge is something that may come with maturity. If children were mature they would not be children. You really can not expect your students to have a "thirst for knowledge."

—

In some schools the students come from homes where parents expect to see good grades on the report card. Students from these homes always do better and are more cooperative. They do not want the teacher to get together with their parents. These adults can not be trusted or controlled by the child in such gatherings. The fact is that both parents usually work full time today; they have less time to investigate the daily or weekly progress of their children. Single parent families exacerbate this problem. The percentage of single parent families is a growing problem in both urban and suburban school systems. These situations allow the children to slack off for a period of time before their parents take notice of it. There are times when students purposely get low grades to get their parents 'attention or as a way of rebellion. Thus even schools in more affluent areas are experiencing a decrease in student motivation.

Fear of failure and the possibility of being held back and separated from friends and classmates is one factor that motivates students to make at least a minimum effort. This does provide some negative motivation for students to work. It is only used sparingly by teachers today. School principals feel that their school is successful when students in their building receive passing grades. These principals are not really concerned whether or not the students have learned the subject matter or are prepared to go on to the next level or grade.

Principals have devised many ways to coerce teachers into giving students passing grades. In most cases, if a teacher has a "higher than average" failure rate then the teacher gets a low rating. If you must remember that average usually means that one half is above and *one half is below* this arithmetic mean. In order to avoid a second low rating, teachers with a higher than average failure rate will grade students differently in order to reduce the number of failures. If all those who had higher than average failure rates reduce their number of failures to just the average of the previous year, then last year's average could be this year's highest failure rate since no one wants to be below this number. This year's average failure rate will be greatly reduced. If you follow this process for a few years, the failure rate will approach zero. This would make everyone happy. The principal could claim that his school is very successful. The parents never complain because their child did not fail. Actual learning declines. This all makes educational good sense if you accept Farber's first postulate. Of course none of this helps the classroom teachers who will be criticized for not doing their job when the SAT scores decline.

Some districts practice "social promotion." There are districts which have a policy that no child will fail more than one grade between first grade and the beginning of high school.[13] Most districts allow a principal to promote a student or students based on the student's age or size. In most districts, the principal has the authority to change any grade given by a child's teacher. Social promotion is used to push kids through the system to save money and the limited resources of the system. It helps to keep politicians and parents happy. I have seen children promoted who missed more than 80% of the school year with unexcused absences. I have seen students skipped from the sixth grade to the ninth grade when some principal

---

13 There is another hidden agenda in this policy. Consider the cost to the district if there were a five percent retention rate every year for ten years. See Farber's seventh postulate.

wanted to get rid of them. All of this tends to destroy the motivation of good students. The students are more aware of these "promotions" than the teachers. We are purposefully kept in the dark because we would object to unearned promotions. The students usually know more about what is going on in the school system than the teachers.

—

So how do you motivate students? First, let's take a good look at your students and try to understand them. Most people like to succeed in things and reap the prestige that comes with success. If people do not think that they can succeed, then they are less likely to try the task. No one can say that you failed at something if you didn't try to do it. This is a rationale that we have all used at one time or another. Students learn this rationale early in their school careers so that by the time you get them they have carved out niches for themselves. Their niche is safe. It is defined by a degree of effort that prevents them from being viewed as an academic failure (in their mind). It also defines their social position in the class. They have areas where they will try and do well. These can be very narrow in some cases but if you look very carefully, all students have them. There are also areas where a student will make only a token effort and expect very little accomplishment but will be satisfied. It is very difficult to get a student to make a true effort to do something if he/she does not really believe that he/she can do it successfully. Adults are no different. Just sit them down at a new computer and watch over their shoulders.

Now ask students to define success. They will usually tell you that it is *getting the maximum return using a minimum of effort.* This is not unlike getting a big return on a small investment. It is considered "smart" when you can do it. In other words, the student doesn't want to work very hard. So what else in new?

So your job as a teacher is to (1) coax them out of their safe little niche and (2) show them how to get large returns on just a little effort.

Before I begin I must warn you never to try anything new with A students. They are succeeding with the present system and can only go down. Changes threaten their position and self-image. They will resent and resist changes. (Aren't these also called "conservatives" in the adult world?) Anyone can teach these students since they want to succeed and will unless the teacher really screws things up.

If you are writing your doctorate dissertation and want to prove a "new" curriculum or method is a better method, always pick a group of A or top track students for your test group. Educational theory is full of such studies that have been statistically proven this way—which is one of the reasons why educational research can't always be trusted.

—

First let's look at some things that may get students out of their niche. One of the best is "*contract*" grades. Most teachers don't use this to full advantage because it puts the student in control. About the only control that teachers' have left are the students' grades. Teachers ask "what would happen to the grade curve under this system?" They ask "what would happen if all the students contracted for and got A's?" My answer to these teachers is that it would be just great if all students succeeded and deserved A's. Success in learning is usually stated as one of the goals of a school system.

A contract grade is a deal signed by the student and the teacher that states specifically what the student must do and what grade will be received if this is done. The student can choose the grade and the work/learning that he/she is willing to do. It is a very good real life lesson for the students. Once a contract is signed, both the parties must keep the agreement. There are times that I have a parent countersign the contract. The teacher is as held by the contract is the student. The lesson is lost if the teacher agrees to re-negotiate the contract.

Let me tell about my best experience with contract grades and the problems it solved. I was required to have nine weeks of ecology in a tenth grade biology course. Ecology is a vast topic that can not really be taught on a high school level in nine weeks. What I did was to divide it into many sub-topics (modules.) Then I came up with articles, books, experiments, film strips, computer disks, etc., which I called "learning modes." There were several learning modes available in each sub-topic. Then I devised what looked like a menu where the students could choose one thing in each sub-topic and use at least one thing in each type of learning mode. They could pick their grade for the grading period by the total number of learning modes completed. Each mode was pass/fail rated upon completion. As students competed modes, they were listed on a large chart posted on one wall of the room. As time progressed, D and C students kept renewing their contracts at higher grades as they realized that if they tried they would succeed. Many A students began to get upset when they realized that former C students were now getting the same grade and could claim the same prestige.

Another method that I've used to get students out of their niche is the *A or F method*. In genetics each student was required to breed and raise two generations of fruit flies to determine the inheritance of some visible trait. This took many weeks and involved observing and recording the traits and sex of hundreds of flies. Since there are so many traits that can be studied in fruit flies, the students were each given different traits to study. Then the student had to write a scientific report of their experiment in acceptable form and grammar. A report was either valid, that is done correctly and worth an A or invalid and thus worthless. The students could do as many rewrites as needed to get the report right as long as it was done by a certain date. It counted as one half of the report card grade for that term. Every year I used several pounds of red ink correcting reports and turning them back to students for rewrites but in the end 98% of the students had an A report and a good grade for the marking period. The infamous fruit fly report became a dreaded annual event.

Then came true success one year when at the beginning of the project, the students announced to me that it was not such a difficult assignment.

They told me that this would be easy. They had talked with the students from other years and discovered the secret of success. They told me that all they had to do was follow directions, and then they *actually* did it right the first time. Not only had they left their niche but discovered how to get an A with a minimum of effort. It was not getting the A that moved them out of the niche, rather that they did not want to do the three or four rewrites that they knew would be necessary, if they did not do it right the first time. Believe me, if there is an easier way of doing something, students will use it. *If you can devise a method whereby doing the task right is the lazy way of doing it, your students will do it right almost all of the time.*

This story leads me to the next thing that is needed to motivate students. Find ways to appeal to their natural laziness. Have you ever known anyone who liked "busy work?" Neither have I. So why do teachers insist in assigning it? Then after assigning it, we have to grade it, which becomes busy work for us.

The policy of one of my schools was that each teacher must assign at least one half hour of work per night per subject or course. That means that each student has at least two and a half hours of work every night-most of it is busy work. Most students either don't do it or copy it from another student. In some classes the assignment is divided up by way of hand motions and notes before the class period is over. Now that students have computers at home, they just run off many copies of the work, changing only the name at the top of the page. And we wonder why students don't learn. I dislike assigning busy work and I know that my students hate to do it, although I can make them turn it in if I place enough grade value on it.

The solution is the *Performance Based Assignment Schedule*. This is something I invented which provided me with an excuse not to assign much homework, and it appeals to the lazy student. I give a test every other week. The grade on that test determines the student's homework assignments for the next two weeks. Students who get above an 85% have no written assignments. Students who get between 76% and 85% have to write out the definitions for the new terms in the chapter. Students who get between 68% and 76% have to do the chapter questions as well as the definitions of the new terms. Students who get below this must outline the chapter as well as doing the questions and terms.

Students learn quickly that the *Performance Based Assignment Schedule* provides them a means to avoid a lot of homework. All they have to do is get good test grades. They quickly discover that it is easier to study for the test than to do all this work. It becomes *slick* to do well on tests since it gets them out of work. The fact that they actually learned the subject in the process is inconsequential to some students.

Laziness is a great motivator. It caused me to invent the *Performance Based Assignment Schedule*. It cuts down on the amount of papers that I must grade each week This also allows me to spend more time with the students who are still outlining the chapter each week. It is then possible to give them the special attention and special assignments to help them learn effectively. It makes both my life and my students lives easier and nicer.

The student who does the work for his/her friends on the computer is usually lazy enough to avoid any serious amount of homework under this plan. This means that the poorer student has to *actually do the assignment* since it can't be copied from other students. This can cause a poor student to suffer a serious side effect—*learning!*

This method serves to separate out the students who are just not trying from those who try but are having some sort of problem. It gives me more time to work individually with the students who are not doing well. This allows me to gain insights into their learning problems so I can help them overcome these problems.

The trick in using such a method is to have some sort of an impressive title for the process. The principal will not know what *Performance Based Assignment Schedule* means and won't ask. Principals usually do not have time to keep up with the latest jargon in each discipline or to read all the educational journals. Of course school administrators will not admit that they are not familiar with the latest educational method or trend, so you will be left alone.

—

Another thing that always happens is that there are some students who will cheat on tests. They are just too lazy to study. This is an easy way to get a grade with little effort. Now truly successful cheating requires quite a bit more planning and thought than most students realize. They must try to figure out what is important and will be asked on the test. They must organize the information, abbreviate or code it, and neatly write it with very small letters in order to get it on the cheat sheet. Actually these are good study skills.

On major tests or unit tests I often allow all students to cheat. I provide each student with an odd colored index card with his/her name on it a day or two before the test. They may use only this card and can put any information on that they think will help them. When the test is over, the card is collected with the test. Truly lazy students will arrive with the card blank the first time that I do this. Other students who do not normally try very hard will seize this opportunity since they believe that they are going to get something for nothing. This makes them try and moves them out of their niche. Those that did not put anything on their cards will suffer put downs from their classmates for being *really* dumb. It is okay to not get passing grades but is not okay (in the adolescent world) not to be street smart. By the third or fourth test of this kind, my students are actually learning to study effectively. Most of them still think that they are getting away with something. Laziness can certainly work wonders.

This procedure also creates a problem for some students. If they prepare the cheat card and do well on the test, they may look like a *nerd*. For many boys this is worse than death. On the other hand, if they do not use the card well, they are not *street smart,* which is almost as bad as being a nerd. It's not easy to be a teenager; they have to make many difficult choices in uncharted waters.

—

There are times that students will work quite hard if they think that they are going to put one over on a teacher or the school. The science fair is one of these events that can bring out the creativity of some of the students who do not normally do much. I do not ask students to do a science project for the fair, I require it. That takes away the *nerd* connotation.

Once again students work hard at trying not to do work. They look for a project that can be done with the least effort, expense, and can create havoc with the school or offend the school. It provides a teacher with a golden opportunity to turn the tables on the students who think they are going to put one over on the system. Students sucker themselves into projects that they thought were non-learning experiences that would be easy and fun. (Read *lazy*) The teacher only has to add a little bit here and twist something there and the project turns into a serious learning experience. The students will never know what hit them until it is too late to turn back.

There was one student a few years ago who asked if condom testing could be her science project. She expected and got a big reaction from the class. She assumed that I would be upset and say no, giving some excuse about what is appropriate in school. (This was before we began to pass out condoms to students as a daily routine) Instead I began to ask her how she planned to measure pressures and volumes of condoms. The other students joined in with suggestions. Before long she had a real scientific study and could not back out of it without losing face. So she completed the project only because it was *easier* than explaining to all her friends why she didn't follow up on her daring project (laziness wins again). She also learned something about how to conduct a controlled experiment. The science fair committee and principal were not too happy about this entry but it was a valid study. They figured that I am crazy anyway and no one really opposes a crazy person since the outcome of such a skirmish can get out of hand.

—

Students always complain that the tests are too difficult. The average or below average students like to take true/false or multiple choice tests. These tests have a security factor for students since they *can answer* every question. (Teachers like these tests because they are quickly corrected and there is usually no argument about which answer is correct) Unfortunately such tests are very language sensitive. That is the student must be able to read well and understand the subtle differences in adjectives and sentence structure. There can be a cross cultural problem with these tests. On a multiple choice test there will be four or five answers. Only one of these is correct. There is usually another answer that is almost, but not quite correct. There is no credit given for picking the "almost" right answer. Thus the student who may know the subject does not get the test grade that really reflects his/her knowledge.

By the time the students reach high school, many of them may have decided that it is impossible for them to get a really good grade on a multiple choice. There are always too many "tricky" answers. They don't really try or study for these types of tests.

The reverse of the almost correct answer is also found on every test. Every question has an answer or two that is ridiculously wrong and can be quickly eliminated by someone who knows the subject. I sometimes give the students the challenge of *answering* one hundred percent of the questions wrong for an automatic A on the test. If they get even one answer correct, they get an automatic D on the test. At first the students think that this will be easy. The lazy students think that they will get an easy A without any study. They joke around saying that this is *really* the test for them. If they can't get an A on this test their friends might think that they are actually a bit slow.

They find out that it is not so easy to get all the questions answered wrong when they don't study and don't read the questions carefully. I then use various modifications to keep them trying. Sometimes I will offer a B for only one right and a C for only three right answers. It does get students to study a bit more and they have to do more analytical thinking. This is because even the poorer students think that it is within their grasp, and thus they will make more effort. It may help them become better test takers in the long run.

—

It is important to have a grading system that matches the objective of the course that you are teaching. Unfortunately in most schools the computer program is only programmed to accommodate one system of grading. There are many courses given in schools where the standard "A, B, C, ..." system does not really fit the objectives of the course. In some courses it may work against the objectives of the course. I first realized this when one school assigned me to teach both biology and health to the same classes. When I was teaching a unit in health about smoking, the objective was to have the students not take up smoking. It didn't really matter if the students could list all the biological effects of smoking on the human body if they smoked anyway. The same students who got good grades in biology did what was necessary to get good grades in health class but it didn't affect their smoking habits.

If you are really going to have open discussions about certain subjects, the students must be able to express themselves without first thinking about how it may affect their grade. In many courses the course object is to change the students' attitude or habits. If it is this type of a course, a "pass/fail" system will work best. The same could be true for a driver education course, a drug education course, an environmental awareness course, a conflict resolution course, sex education course, etc. Again, the common thread of these courses is that they have as their primary objective is a change in the students' attitude or habits.

Most school administrators will not allow courses to have a different grading system. The way a classroom teacher can get around this is to give everyone who passes the course an "A." There is usually not an administration objection to high grades since they will not get any student or parent complaints about them. In the rare cases where an administrator may object to too many A grades, give every student who passes a B and give an A to any student that does some sort of special report or project.

This type of system often results in getting more cooperation of the students and they enjoy having a course without the competitive pressure from the high achievers. The students think that they are getting an *easy* grade but as long as the teacher keeps the minimum work for passing at a reasonable level, they will all learn as much or even more than they would have under a traditional grading system.

—

Schools have forgotten that one of the objectives of a grade is to communicate the progress or accomplishments of the student to the student, the parent, a potential employer, or to a person representing another educational institution. Each of these four different people is looking for different types of information. The level of sophistication of each of these is different. There are many terms and standards that are unique to educators but would be either misunderstood or meaningless to employers. In keeping with Farber's first postulate, schools normally use a grading system that does not really tell any of these groups what they need to know. To do otherwise would be intelligent. There is no school system that is willing to have more than one system simultaneously just to better communicate to both employers and universities. This would take work! Laziness will always point the way. This postulate has very broad implementations. It has application far beyond education.

Stop for a moment and think about how ridiculous it is to sum up all the work, all the topics studied and all the different things that you learned in a year-long course with only one letter of the alphabet. All of this accomplishment does not even get one entire word! A course syllabus is never included in a school transcript or in the student's permanent record. The course title is almost never more than two words and in many cases it is just a department course number.

Employers need to know the student's ability in specific skills. If a person is being considered for an office type of job, the employer could make a better decision if a transcript listed such things as typing (keyboarding) speed rather than a letter grade in typing. The same is true of the technical skills. How good is the auto shop student at a brake job, a valve job, or electronic diagnostic systems? The student would not need to be good at all of these to get a job with many auto service centers but could get a job if the employer had reliable information as to the student's specific skills. A letter grade in auto shop does not tell the employer enough to make a good decision. The same could be said of all the technical fields.

Most employers want to know about the person's reliability. The school transcript usually does not include anything about student lateness and/or absences. Nor does it tell the employer anything about the student's ability to work with people and get along with others. It would be better to have a list of skills and a report that communicates the student's performance in these areas. For instance a report may tell an employer that the student's skill in operating a milling machine is accurate within specific tolerances.

Colleges and universities are more interested in the student's scores on standardized achievement tests in specific subjects as well as overall reading and math skills. Think of a B grade in eleventh grade English. What does this tell the college? It does not tell the college anything about the writing skill or even the reading skill of the student. Every high school's eleventh grade English course is different in some way from the same course in another high school. Many colleges use the class rank of the student as an evaluation because they don't know how the actual letter grades relate to the ability of the student.[14]

---

14 Some parents will transfer their child from a very completive "magnet" high school to a less competitive school to enable the student to graduate in the top of the class. This will make it easier for the student to be accepted into a particular college or win a scholarship.

Another reason that such a system is not used is that the school could not just list a course title and a grade on a transcript. The school system likes to be able to have the entire student transcript on one side of a single sheet of 8" by 11" paper. School administrators, secretaries, etc. are human too, and therefore are motivated by the same factor as students: *laziness*.

And yet another reason that most schools would not permit such a system is because it does not allow the computation of class standings. It is important to the better ranked students to have a large numbers of students below them even if these students are not college bound and therefore not in competition with the high ranking students. Every so often a student who took a business or industrial arts curriculum will have an average that places him or her first in the graduating class. It is fun to watch the academic staff revise the ranking system to prevent this student from being ranked first in the class. The result is that most schools have a course or grade weighting system that prevents someone taking industrial or business courses from graduating first in the class. This is done by counting an A as 4.2 rather than a 4 when it is earned in an honors course or an accelerated course.

This is one of the many subtle ways that the school destroys the motivation of some students.

There are many others.

—

I was teaching in a school system that refused to send home a report card that told the parents the progress of the student for a particular nine week marking period or quarter. It sends home *only* the cumulative grade for student going back to the first day of school in September. It works this way. If a student does C in the first quarter, a C appears on the first quarter report card. If the student then does A work the second quarter, a B appears on the second report card. The actual result is that unless the student gets an A the first quarter, it is rare for the student to receive an A on a report card. These children seldom have as many A's to show off to relatives and friends as students in other school districts. The cumulative effect is that these urban students develop poor self-images. The teachers have presented logical and intelligent reasons to the" powers that be" to change the system. Of course, logic and intelligence has no effect on educational systems. It is more convenient for school administrators to have look at only one grade to see his/her over all progress rather than figure an average of the grades earned over two or three quarters of the course. This is just plain laziness on the part of the central administrative offices. Meanwhile the district annually spends tens of thousands of dollars on teacher in-service workshops on how *teachers* can better motivate their students.

One way around this is to post the names of students who have earned A's and/or B's for the quarter or for a unit on posters around the classroom. One of the things that high school and college teachers seem to forget is that students like to see their good work and their name posted around the school. All people respond to what is generally known in education as "positive reinforcement."

—

P.T. Barnum said that" there is a sucker born every minute." I believe he also was the one that said that "you can't cheat an honest man." He understood human nature and I'm sure he would agree with me that laziness has been given a bum rap in this country. It provides the driving force in our great nation and yet is never touted as a virtue. People work tremendously hard all of their lives so that they can retire and do nothing. People are always looking for an easier way of doing their work and invent all sorts of mechanical and electronic systems to be able to make their work easier. They develop procedures: change the layout of work stations, etc. to streamline the job that needs to be done. Only the truly stupid complain about inventions, methods and procedures that save *work*.

A successful teacher must take a lesson from P.T. Barnum. Every lazy student is a sucker for something that seems to be the easy way out.

Students usually know what they can do well and what is difficult for them to do. The truly lazy student only wants to do what he or she does well particularly if they can see a choice of doing one or the other. (They often would prefer to do nothing so that is not an option offered). When students are offered the choice of doing a portfolio where they get to choose the type of work that they can put into it, this is the bait that many students will take. (This will also work for projects) These students will figure that they will fill the portfolio with things that are easy for them to do. What they really don't realize is that there may be a hook in the portfolio. A portfolio is usually an open ended situation.

Next you get the students to do a first piece for their portfolio. Then you let them know that they should do better on the next piece. Little by little you keep refining and expanding their work which requires them to learn new things and expand their horizons. The additional requirements must be such that the student never perceives the change as more than a wee little bit of additional work. Before long you can have them doing work of a better quality and at a higher level that they never intended to do or thought that they could do. By the time that student discovers that he/she has done much more work than intended it is too late to quit. To stop building the portfolio or project at this point would be cheating one's self out of getting credit for all this work. That would be dumb in the eyes of one's classmates and so now peer pressure is working against laziness. So they keep adding and building their portfolio.

Having students develop a portfolio as a way of teaching is not something that lends itself to every situation and student. A teacher must recognize when and with whom it will work and when it will not work. Being a teacher or a con man is an art. It requires the same skills and understanding of human nature.

—

Laziness is not the only force that motivates students. All those education-al methods courses that told you that students would learn if you could devise ways to make learning fun were not wrong. Many of these things will work well with "normal" students. However, this presents the novice teacher with two problems.

First is that the new teacher is usually given the classes that no ex-perienced teacher wants to try to teach. These classes contain either the most disruptive students in the grade or the slowest students. Usually the class is a deadly combination of both. In other words, your classes are not the normal type of class that you were trained to teach. If you turn the lesson into a game, the disruptive students do what they are best at doing and make it next to impossible for the class to benefit from the educational game. These disruptive students apply pressure on the other students not to work or cooperate with the teacher. The teacher must first get the disruptive on his/her side. When these students think that they are putting one over on the teachers, they work smoothly. Anytime they think that they have found a method to get an easy grade or a good grade for almost nothing, they will go for it. Methods that appeal to their lazi-ness will usually work.

The second problem is that not the entire curriculum that you will be required to teach is fun stuff. Some of it is downright obsolete and tedious. Any teacher but especially a novice teacher is going to be hard put to come up with enough ways to make these areas into anything that is fun or in-teresting. Parents and the public in general will point to the educational programs on television and tell you that this is what you should be doing in your classroom. These programs are usually interesting and cleverly done. You can do the same thing in your class if you are given the tens of thousands or hundreds of thousands of dollars and many man-hours that are spent on every half hour of television programming. If you can show the students an easy way to get through this *"boring stuff" you* can have them tamed and eating out of your hand.

Another problem is that what one person considers fun or interesting will be dull or boring to another person. It is difficult to motivate everyone in an average class. The school year is usually at least hundred and eighty days long. There are going to be times that you run out of ideas and energy to keep the lessons fresh and exciting. You will realize that you have days that you feel like taking it easy on yourself. That is when you will realize that laziness is a motivating force in your life also. It is a universal force that shapes our lives and life styles. Today's teacher has very few tools left to deal with students who are in school only because the law requires them to attend school. Teaching is a subversive occupation.[15] Don't be afraid to subvert the students' natural laziness to the cause of education.

---

15 Teachers are part of a system that is often trying to change society and the country via their students. This is explained in Chapter 10.

CHAPTER 4

Farber's Fourth Postulate

IT IS BETTER TO GIVE THAN RECEIVE, SO GIVE EVERYBODY A ROUGH TIME

How many of us really remember what we did in school? Do you remember that really nice patient teacher that all the students took advantage of? They made this person's life miserable even though most of the students really liked this teacher. I remember saying, when I was in high school, that I would never consider being a teacher because I would never take the stuff that we did to our teachers.

Well, can you at least remember when someone put a tack on the teacher's chair?

In my over four decades of teaching, I have known many teachers who were tormented unmercifully by their students. There are other teachers that the same students wouldn't dare do anything to aggravate. The difference had nothing to do with their dedication or knowledge of their subject. Students do not necessarily respect teachers for professional expertise or dedication. The same is often true of school administrators.

The first year of my teaching career I was teaching an eighth grade science class and I brought in a couple of boxes of expensive chocolates to show and later share with the more adventurous students. I had a box on my desk when the first class arrived but like a good teacher I supervised the hallway until the late bell. I started my lesson and when I got to the part where I was going to use the candy I discovered that the box was totally empty. The students never miss a thing. They had taken and eaten every single piece of individually foil wrapped candy. As I looked closer I realized that there were foil wrappers scattered throughout the room. All the students knew that the candy had been stolen. The students were quiet as they waited anxiously for my reaction to their thievery. What is this "newbie" teacher going to do? Make a fool of himself by going to the principal? Try to punish the whole class when he couldn't prove who was guilty and innocent? Would he just wimp out and go on to something else until the class does something else to him? This is a moment of truth for a class.

Fortunately I had put another box of candy away in a closet so I got it out and showed them the four varieties of chocolate covered insects- ants, caterpillars, bees and beetles. At this point a number of students turned rather green and needed to go to the lavatory due to upset stomachs.

Both the students and I learned a valuable lesson. It was not the lesson that I had so carefully planned. The students learned never to take anything from my desk and I learned that it is better to give than receive.

—

This incident made me aware of another problem that I would repeatedly face in teaching and I would soon learn another valuable lesson as I attempted to solve it.

It seems that I was required to be in two places at the same time. If not physically in two places, at least in control of the students who were in two separate places—the hallway and my classroom. Since Farber's first postulate had not yet been discovered, I took a logical approach. I made an appointment with the principal and went into his office to explain that it was not logical to expect a teacher to be able to control all the actions of all the students in two different areas at the same time. I could not be supervising in the hallway and see/supervise the actions of students in my science classroom. Since there are always things which are potentially dangerous in a science classroom, I believed there was a problem.

He listened politely and then gave me one of those all-knowing fatherly smiles and told me that good teachers figure out how to do this. In his opinion, I had the potential to be a really good teacher when I got enough experience. (This is the way of getting around having me ask any more logical questions). He appreciated my concerns but told me that I shouldn't worry because this is just the way things are done in school. "You will understand all this in time."

Unfortunately for the principal, this was not my first job out of college. I had spent a couple of years in industry and seen a bit of the "real world." If it smells like bull, looks like bull and bellows like bull, it is a sure bet that it is "bull." I well understood the lubricating value of B.S. I had come to understand the value of this special lubricant in keeping business, sales, and industry operating. I also knew that there are times and places where it doesn't work. The plant where I had worked had five workers killed and numerous workers injured in the couple of years that I was employed there. I had seen what happens when there is an accident. Believe me, I have seen some outstanding bull artists in my industrial experience. I also had observed where the axe fell when there was an accident that could not be covered up with bull. The education business appeared to be no different. I decided early on that the axe wasn't going to land on me!

One of the first things a successful person learns in business or government work is when and how to "CYA" *(cover your ass).*

It was memo time. Interesting enough, memos seem to cause more of a reaction in education than they do in business. It may be due to the fact that very few teachers take the time or feel the need to write them since they tend to be trusting people. Or it could be that for all the talk about writing across education, educators are fearful about writing themselves. In any case, administrators have not built up the resistance to memos and are not adept at passing them off.

I sent the principal a simple memo stating that I did not know how to supervise students and therefore could not accept responsibility for all the actions of the students in both places. I went on to explain that I would be willing to continue being in and supervising the hallway during class change if he would just sign a statement accepting liability for all accidents that may occur in the science room or class that may be due to students tampering with chemicals, equipment, etc. while I was in the hallway.

It was kind of like a bomb went off downstairs.[16] The principal assured me that the school would back me 100% in case of an accident. He said that there was no need to have a signed statement. No teacher had ever asked for a signed statement before. It was unprofessional. Since backing is assured, there is no need to have anything in writing. Professionals don't put things in writing. That is part of being a professional. This circular ill-logic continued until he noticed that like a good student that I had taken out my notebook and was taking notes.

"What are you doing?" He asked.

"Taking notes." I replied.

"Why"

"Because I want to be sure that I remember everything that you told me."

"Other teachers don't take notes."

"My science background has taught me not to trust my memory but to record things immediately"

"It is not necessary. I don't understand your attitude. That is an administrative function." With that our meeting was abruptly concluded.

I typed up the notes with the principal's statement that he would not sign a statement accepting liability and could not tell me how I could supervise the activities of students in two places at the same time but was still requiring me to do this. I then sent him the notes of our meeting to sign or

---

16 The science department is almost always located on the top floor. It is rumored that this is so because officials don't have much faith in the sanity of science teachers. If a science demonstration or experiment causes an explosion, only the roof will be lost. It is more likely due to the fact that odors tend to rise upward with the air currents of the building and science labs generate many unusual scents. Science teachers claim that this topography reflects their proper position in the academic world.

initial if they were correct. I asked him to make any corrections if needed and then initial the correction notes.

I expected another explosion but this time he came to me. (This is most unusual since administrators usually get nose bleeds due to the fact they are not used to the altitude of the upper floors of the school building where the science department is located.) He told me that since I was inexperienced and timid, it would be better if I just supervised my classroom during class change and let the other teachers supervise the hallways.

It is better to give than receive when it comes to chiefs as well as with the Indians. I learned to give everyone a rough time before they gave it to me. It is an ability that may be a key in surviving in education with your sanity still intact.

This same principal had given me some excellent advice on my first introduction to the school. He told me that it is more important for students to respect me than to like me. He said that students will learn to like and appreciate such teachers. They will fondly remember those teachers who were demanding and not those who let them get away with things.

Two and a half years later I was made science department head (maybe it was better to be respected) and shortly thereafter I demanded that all my science teachers be excused from hallway duty during class change.

I should note that this principal, Mac, and I became good friends and kept in contact long after he retired. It turned out that he also was one who gave rather than received. He pushed his students beyond what they wanted to do or believed that they could do. They seemed to emerge from his tutelage with more backbone and self-confidence. In his later years he got notes and memos of appreciation from students who had found success in all walks of life. He never knew where they would turn up. Once he was rushed to a hospital for an emergency operation. The surgeon came out and introduced himself just before the operation. Mac took a look at the doctor and said "Aren't you that bonehead that used to sit in the back of my senior English class?" At this point the doctor realized who this old man was and a lasting friendship was formed.

—

At this point I need to point out that there is a difference between practicing Farber's fourth postulate to protect yourself from receiving a rough time from others and making enemies. People usually know when they are out of line and deserve to be given a rough time. If on the other hand, you just give people a rough time without good reason, you will lose in the long run.

—

At many schools there is a *business manager or purchasing manager* who oversees the purchasing of all the supplies and equipment. The people in this position often are not concerned about getting the supplies in a timely fashion and often make substitutes without consulting the teachers. The results can be disruptive to the educational program.

Early in my teaching career, the business manager did not order the fish to be dissected by my biology class. He didn't feel that it was necessary to tell me, a lowly teacher, that he did not order the fish. When it came to the time to dissect the fish and the fish had not arrived, there was a problem. I went to his office to complain. I was told that the fish order was not cost efficient. The containers and shipping costs were more than the fish and that if I wanted fish, I would have to order this in a much larger quantity to make it cost efficient. He told me that he could buy them at the supermarket at a lower price.

I had only one class of about 25 students in biology so I went to the supermarket and got a dozen whole fresh fish for the class to dissect. As in many schools, trash cans are emptied only when they are full. This was another of the efficiencies of the business manager's office. I did not want to have the smell of fish in my room or hallway. I took the remains of the fish to the trash receptacle in the hallway outside of the business manager's office. This was an area that was not frequented by students. Within a day or two the decaying fish produced a strong odor in this hallway. The trash can was emptied even though it was not full. The odor lingered even after the can was emptied. The business manager was quite upset with me.

I explained to him that (1) had he purchased the preserved fish for my class to dissect, they would not have decayed and produced such smell (2) that he had indicated to me where to get the fish and (3) that fish could not have been disposed of in an area frequented by students because the students and their parents would have caused problems for the administration. I then reminded him that he had saved the school the expense of buying fish since I had paid for the fish.

I don't recall ever having trouble with the purchase orders for biological supplies again until this man retired.

—

When I was working in a boarding school, I was responsible for getting all of the students to dinner on time. Students were not allowed to miss meals or be late for grace. The students had to be properly dressed for the meal. This meant that they were wearing long pants, shirts and dress shoes (not sandals or athletic shoes). The normal procedure was to ring the bell in the dormitory ten minutes before a meal. The students were normally on time and properly dressed.

Then there was Harry! Harry could sleep through anything. Actually I don't think that a cherry bomb would have disturbed his sleep. The fire alarm bell certainly did not bother him. His roommate would yell at him and shake him. Harry would finally reply, "Okay, I'm getting up in a minute," and promptly fall back to sleep. The only thing that woke Harry was when the dorm got quiet. Then he would jump up, step into his sandals and run to the dining hall. He always arrived in sandals. His excuse was that he did not have time to put on dress shoes.

I tried to reason with Harry. He was a nice guy, but I couldn't permit him to continue to be late to meals and violate the dress code. I couldn't get him to change his ways. I wanted to find a way of getting Harry to change his ways without resorting to formal punishment.

One day I had the students on either side of Harry's room turn up their stereo to a volume a bit louder than normal.[17] Then I proceeded to fasten Harry's sandals to the floor with roofing nails. That evening at dinner Harry came in later than usual. He was wearing leather shoes as specified in the dress code and his face was bright red. He angrily told me that he jumped out of bed as usual into his sandals and promptly fell flat on his face when he tried to walk. One sandal came apart while the other remained steadfast to the floor. The entire dining hall had a good laugh.

Harry did amend his ways somewhat. His rebut to me was that his sandals were never the same and that I had ruined them. He has never forgotten the incident. If I were to meet him today, some twenty-plus years later, I'm sure that he would remind me of his sandals.

—

One of the problems that I encountered as science department head at one school was the use of the science department and its equipment by the summer school staff. For some strange reason, the school chose not to hire any of the regular staff for the summer program. All the teachers were from outside of our school system and thus could not really be held accountable for things.

I was told that all of the keys to the science rooms were to be turned into the high school office and that the keys to the storage and supply closets and cabinets were to be placed in an area that was clearly marked for the summer school staff. I realized that there could be some problems and requested that I be given a list of science equipment and supplies that the summer school teachers would be needing rather than having them going

---

17 *Normal music* for teenagers far exceeds OSHA limits for safety in heavy industry. School employees are not protected by OSHA regulations.

through all the equipment areas.

The request for a list was ignored and the summer school staff was given free rein to go through the science department and use what they wanted. When we returned in September, we found that a four year supply of preserved frogs had been used (I guess that students dissected a frog every day till they did it right) and a microscope had been destroyed. Since microscopes are expensive and we did not have extra money in our budget to replace it, I was a bit upset.

The next year I again made the request that I be given a list of science supplies and equipment that would be needed by the summer school staff. Again my request was ignored and I was told just to leave the keys to the supply and equipment storage area where the summer school staff could find them.

In my biology classroom I had installed an observation beehive. The hive had one side that was made of glass so that the students could observe the activities of the bees in the hive. The bee hive was connected by a pipe that went outside of the building at the bottom of a classroom window. The bees flew in and out of the hive throughout the daylight hours during the warm weather. In the summertime the hive contained several thousand bees.

I placed the keys to all the supply and equipment storage areas inside of the glass beehive. The keys were in plain sight and to my way of thinking, readily available to a knowledgeable science teacher. The keys were still in the hive when we returned in the fall and our science supplies and equipment was all intact.

The third year I did not have to request a list of supplies and equipment from the summer school staff. A request for supplies and equipment appeared as part of the normal planning for the summer school program. From this point on the summer staff and the science department had a good relationship and we were supportive of each other.

You may wonder about the problems of keeping a bee hive in a classroom. Once bees are acclimated to a new hive, they will leave and enter the hive without any problems. Their navigation is excellent. I was able to teach my classes in the spring and fall with the other windows wide open without any bees flying into the classroom.

In most neighborhoods there are several bee hives. I took the trouble to locate and point out several hives of wild bees for my students. The students thought that I could tell the difference between wild bees and the bees in the classroom. I did nothing to dissuade their belief. I told them if they were ever stung by a bee, bring it in and I would tell them if it was one of my bees.

—

This same boarding school hired a new headmaster who had no boarding school experience. He was a great practitioner of Farber's fourth postulate. Sometimes he didn't always think things through completely before he made and published policy changes.

On one occasion some students came to him and said that they needed more privacy from the house parent staff. The house parents had pass keys to all the students' rooms. The students wanted to put dead bolt locks that could only be opened from the inside of their rooms.

Without consulting anyone, he decreed that the students could put locks on their doors so that they would not be disturbed by the house parents. He went on to make some statements about the right to privacy etc. This was in a boarding school that went from first grade through high school.

Since I was in charge of one of the dormitories, this immediately impacted on my job. I immediately replied to this decree with a memo (copies to the appropriate offices) that my staff and I could not be responsible for students using alcohol, smoking materials, drugs, etc. in their rooms since we no longer had access. I then went on to request a fire ax and sledge hammer for each of the house parent staff so that we might be able to rescue students from burning rooms. (The student rooms had heavy fire proof doors that stood up to all kinds of student abuse.)

Needless to say, the policy quickly reverted back to the original system. The next time dormitory policy changes were contemplated, the headmaster consulted with some of the dormitory staff first.

—

One of my new science teachers had a boy in class who absolutely refused to cooperate with the teachers. I had to remove the boy from the classroom and I put him in my room. This was a last period class so I decided the best thing to do was to keep the boy after school as a punishment.

This boy made it quite clear to me, my class and anyone else within hearing range that he was not going to wash the board, do school work or anything else. I might be able to make him stay after school but that was all that I could do. He then informed the world that he was leaving in just one hour.

He was good to his word. He would not do anything so I made him sit facing the back of the room. He promptly fell asleep. I woke him. He fell asleep again. I could not even get him to stay awake. He did however manage to wake himself up to look at the wall clock about every fifteen minutes.

I waited until he was asleep again and began turning the wall clock back. In ten or twelve minute increments, I managed to get the clock turned back about an hour and one half. Finally the clock read four thirty and the boy promptly got up and left the room. It was actually almost six o'clock.

The boy always gave me a strange look after that day and tried to avoid me. He did decide to behave in science class but got in trouble in most other classes. He somehow avoided ever being in one of my classes.

—

One of the things that makes new teachers very uneasy is when a principal or vice principal sits in on the class. It is best to remain in charge of the classroom. It may be small but it is your domain and you are in charge of all the people in the room. With this attitude you can treat an administrator as a student and have him or her participate in class. While some administrators will not always cooperate, many like to have the chance to interact with the students or more likely, they don't know how to refuse to interact with the class. This is not giving them a rough time, but focusing their attention on what your class is all about. If you don't do this, you will find that they will be reporting on the posters on the walls or how neat you keep your desk, etc. If you do this the first time that you are visited, the frequency of visits will usually drop off sharply.

In one school my very first administrative visit was by a vice principal who was unlucky enough to enter my class at the beginning of a two period chemistry lab. I immediately made him a member of a lab team (the experiments in this school were always done in groups of three or four). This was a two person group that needed another person to fill the group. The two boys in this group were the class brains. This was why no one wanted to be in their group. The boys knew far more chemistry that this administrator so he had to try to bluff his way through the experiment or let the students direct his activities. Once the lab started, he could not leave until the experiment was completed and the lab report written up and turned in to me. I don't think that he had intended to spend two periods in my class. At the end of the lab he told me that he enjoyed the class.

Most administrators appreciate a teacher who takes charge and once they realize that you are in charge of your class and serious about your lesson, they don't feel the need to visit your classroom very often.

—

We have all heard about or experienced pressure from coaches who want special treatment for their athletes. Most schools have eligibility rules for sports teams. Unfortunately schools get more publicity from the performance of their sports teams than academic success. This makes sports more important than scholarship in 99% of educational institutions (refer to Farber's first postulate). Star college athletes are given light loads with easy instructors while teachers of high school stars are pressured to make exceptions to their normal grading system.

I am maybe the only teacher that ever called the football coach to demand that an exception be made for a boy to be on the football team. The coach immediately told me that this boy had tried out and was big enough but didn't know much about football. My reply was that he was in my biology class also and didn't come knowing much biology. Isn't our job to teach the subjects? I then went to that athletic director and the building principal and repeated my request. Nobody had ever made a request like this before. They didn't know what to do, so they took the easy way out and put him on the JV football team.

As Paul Harvey used to say, "Here is the rest of story. I was teaching in an academic magnet school that had very high academic admission standards, but still was able to consistently produce winning sports teams in all areas. My freshman biology class included a tall boy who seemed very bright but immediately distinguished himself by not turning in acceptable assignments. I immediately decided to call his parents to nip the problem early and/or CYA when the boy received a failing grade in biology. To my surprise, I discovered that this boy was living in a children's shelter. In my conversations with the boy, he expressed that he didn't like all the work required by this school and wanted to go to his local neighborhood school. In that school the dropout rate was deplorable and even those who graduated often lacked basic reading and math skills. He needed a reason to do the work and learning, which we required in this school. A freshman who makes the football team is immediately a "big-man-on-campus." This makes the individual popular with girls and respected by the guys. However, one can not stay on the team with failing grades. And yes, I gave him a rough time throughout the biology course. He grudgingly did enough work and studying to get by during football season. By then he was hooked and did not want to be forced back to his neighborhood high school.

The boy maintained the lowest average possible to keep his athletic eligibility, made the varsity team the next three years, graduated and started college on a combination of athletic and need scholarships.

—

In one school I was assigned to be on the curriculum study committee. This is not a task most experienced teachers volunteer to do but each department wants be represented on this committee. This is one of those thankless and usually unproductive jobs that teachers must do from time to time.

This is a committee which spends a lot of time reviewing the present curriculum, then the curriculum of other schools, then accept suggestions for change from committee members and school faculty and finally ends up in a very heated debate as every academic department tries to protect its turf. Usually the committee avoids making any significant changes but decides that it needs to study the suggested changes more and gather more information ... In a year or two the process will start over again. In rare cases the committee actually makes significant changes.

This was my first experience on this school's committee. It gave me an opportunity to develop an understanding of the overall school program and the history of how the program and specific course offerings had been developed.

One of the most interesting courses was a speech course which was a required course for all seniors. The existence of this course requirement limited the number of electives that a senior could select. Several departments wanted to offer another elective course at the senior level but there was no hope of filling such courses since all the seniors had to take this speech course. It seems obvious that the speech course requirement could be dropped or changed to a sophomore or junior level course. The English chairman just smiled at the suggestion. He did not argue or say anything about the suggestion. A few other senior teachers on the committee listened patiently and then simply told us (the new teachers) that it can't be changed.

This was news to us. We thought that the job of the committee was to study the curriculum and make changes as the committee deemed necessary.

That is true to an extent. But the speech course is Dr. B's course and this is the way that he wants it. The curriculum committee could not make any curriculum changes that affected Dr. B.

It seems that Dr. B was the speech teacher and in charge of the theater department. It was a two person department. Dr. B put on two very outstanding plays a year and a part of the weekly assembly program. He was trouble with a capital T when he did not get his way. He had a booming voice that he could project across any auditorium. He would go over anyone's head to get his way. He would go to the school board, parents, etc. when necessary. No one wanted to cross him. He knew how to give everyone a rough time so he was left alone. Our small graduating classes had produced a number of actors and public figures. We had one graduate of this high school that very year that was doing the newscast on a local station just a few weeks after graduation. Dr. B produced good results but was demanding. Not every student wanted to take up a career in this area, but had to take his course anyway. We had to wait until he retired to change the curriculum to allow our seniors more elective courses.

—

One of the problems all teachers have is being able to bring things into the classroom to display without having the students handling (and eventually destroying) these objects of interest. It seems that when students ask to see something they really mean that they want to handle it. Unless you are teaching in the school for the blind, this becomes a problem. This is especially true in science classes where the teacher may have chemicals on the table set up for a demonstration. The problem is compounded when a teacher is assigned to teach two or more different science courses. The teacher has only one preparation period to set up for the day so that there will be objects that may arouse student curiosity that are set up for a different course.

Students must be trained to look but not to touch things that they do not understand unless they are invited by the teacher to handle the object. They must learn not to touch anything on the teacher's desk. This is something that I have tried to teach every year. My success rate in teaching this varies from year to year. Students in general learn from experience better than they learn from oral or written communications.

One of the things which is easily made is a buzzing box.[18] This consists of a battery operated buzzer with a motion switch (mercury switch) that begins to buzz when a student moves it and can not be turned off by the student. The teacher leaves it on the his/her desk. The students are warned not to handle anything on the desk. Usually it does not sit on the desk for more than a class period or two before a student picks it up. Then you get to watch a student try to tell you that he or she didn't do anything or touch anything when you and everyone else in the class know otherwise.

Another version of the buzzing box uses a light activated switch (photocell) which is placed in the teacher's desk drawer. Students often try to sneak into this drawer to snitch hall passes, see the grade record book, or look for test answer keys. Other times they just want a pencil or a paper clip. Sometimes it is hard to get students just to ask for school supplies. After a couple of students are embarrassed by the buzz box, the students are more likely to ask for things rather than just going into the teacher's desk.

The problem of having living specimens in the biology classroom is a

---

18 Instructions, parts and sometimes kits for these simple devices are available in electronics catalogues and stores such as Radio Shack. Sometimes I have the students build these things as part of an electrical unit in a general science class.

particular challenge. Aside from students harming the living plant or animal, there is also the hazard of the student being infected by something in an animal's cage or aquarium. The first thing you learn is to put secure covers on all cages and aquariums. Students will drop or pour things through anything that has a screen top unless it is on a high shelf. Glass or Plexiglas tops are best for fish tanks. Small warning signs on cages often are effective. A sign the reads "biting mouse" or "this snake is *usually* non-poisonous" makes the students think.

I had a live tarantula in my classroom for several years. On its aquarium there was a small sign that read "In case of emergency call -"and then there was a business card from a funeral home about two blocks from the school. The students would ask me if the tarantula was really poisonous and dangerous. I would tell them that all tarantulas are poisonous (true) and that for most people the bite is not serious *BUT* one out of twelve people may be allergic to the poison (also true) and these people can have a fatal reaction. I then told them that the only way to know if they were the one out of twelve was to have the tarantula bite them. In all the years that I had the tarantula, as far as I know, no student ever opened the cage. No one ever wanted to find out if they were allergic to the poison.

—

In my seventh grade life science classes I used to do an elaborate demonstration about the effects of smoking cigarettes. This demonstration was a controlled experiment. One goldfish would be the smoker and the other would be the nonsmoker. Using a pump system one fish would be aerated with normal air and the other fish would be aerated with a mixture of air and cigarette smoke. I had several students help me perform this experiment in front of the class. I usually picked students who I knew or suspected were smokers. By the end of the class period, the goldfish who was the smoker would be showing obvious signs of distress. I would then give this fish to someone in the class to take home as a pet while keeping the healthy fish in the classroom.

Of course I had to buy cigarettes and bring them into the classroom to conduct this experiment. I knew there was a chance that some student would take some of the cigarettes. I went to the local novelty store and purchased "cigarette loads" which are a little stick that is put in the non-filter end of cigarettes that causes the cigarette to explode. I marked the cigarettes that I needed for the demonstration and loaded the others.

One time when the demonstration was completed and class was over I counted my loaded cigarettes and found that two were missing. I thought that I had been watchful but somehow the hand is faster than the eye. I wondered which of my assistants had taken them and what had happened. Five and a half years later on graduation day some students drew me aside to tell me the story.

It seems that the boy who was the class bully, and who had been one of the students who were helping me with the demonstration, was the one who had taken the cigarettes. Immediately after class he bragged to the class that he had taken Farber's cigarettes. He then took his audience into the lavatory to smoke them. He made a big show of lighting up a cigarette and puffing it. On the third puff it blew up. At that point the class was laughing at him instead of with him.

My reputation was made with this class. I had earned their respect. I had many of these same students later in both my biology and chemistry courses and they were some of my better students.

—

One problem that every teacher encounters is student complaints about their grades. No matter how contentious a teacher is about clearly marking papers, quizzes and tests, students will claim not to understand their grade. At the end of a marking period the student will claim that he or she deserves a higher grade because of an A on one quiz and ignoring the F's on three major tests. Students like to argue with an encouraging audience of students who know that if one student wins a grade change, all the other students will have a better chance of pressing for a change.

The solution to this problem is Farber's official *Student Grade Complaint form.* This is an official looking form complete with a school form number that is given to any student who has a complaint about his or her grade. The student is instructed to complete three copies of the form and keep one, give one to the teacher and the last to the department chairman. Incomplete forms are not acceptable and all spelling, grammar and punctuation must be correct for the form to be given consideration.

Over the years I have handed out many of these forms to my students. I can count the number that were fully completed and turned back to me on one hand. Yes, once in a while I have recorded an incorrect number for a test score or have made a math error. When I began to use a computer to keep records and calculate grades, the math errors disappeared so at least no one questions the math ability of the computer. At most the students just ask to have a printout of their grades that were entered in the computer.

The first year that I was a teacher, I was frustrated that I was not getting the same results from my students as the biology teacher next door. I wanted to find out what I was doing different. I made arrangements to sit in the back of this teacher's class on my free periods. After several days of this I was even more confused. I was having trouble staying awake in his class while the students seem to hang on his every word. He spoke slowly and meticulously, pointing out the smallest details of what was being studied.

Finally I asked him "what is the secret of keeping the students so well behaved and attentive?"

He replied that a teacher "had to have the patience of a saint and the disposition of a despot." At the time I really didn't understand what he meant. Only later, as I developed this postulate, did I understand what he told me. He could be the student's best friend and most patient instructor, but if you ever crossed him, you would have more trouble than you could handle. He was one of the most successful teachers that I ever had the pleasure of knowing.

Form rf-04-88

STUDENT GRADE COMPLAINT—Science

Student _____
            (last)   (first)   (M.I.)

Homeroom/Advisory number _____

Parent/guardian _____
            (last)   (first)

Address _____

_____

Phone (home) _____ (work) _____

Teacher _____

Course _____ period _____

Textbook title _____

Textbook author _____

Copyright date _____ Textbook number _____

Grade _____ Behavior Rating _____ Report Period _____

Grade previous report period _____

No. of days absent (total for year) _____ (total this report period) _____

Number of times late to class this report period _____

What did you do to make up work missed due to absences? _____

_____

Percent of assignments completed satisfactorily _____%

Number of lab reports completed this report period _____

Grades of lab reports 1. ___ 2. ___ 3. ___ 4. ___ 5. ___ 6. ___ 7. ___

Number of tests given this report period _____

Grades of tests you have taken 1. ___ 2. ___ 3. ___ 4. ___ 5. ___

Did you do any extra credit work? _____ If "yes," describe the work.

_____

_____

[SIDE 2]

Is there any reason that you should be given special consideration? _____

If "yes," write a paragraph describing the conditions that warrant this consideration. _____

_____

_____

_____

_____

_____

_____

The space below is for you to write a paragraph (or more) explaining what grade you should receive and how you earned this grade. If you need more space, you may attach additional pages to this form.

_____

_____

_____

_____

_____

_____

_____

_____

_____

_____

Date _____

Signature _____

CHAPTER 5

Farber's Fifth Postulate

"SUCCESS" IN THE TEACHING PROFESSION IS NOT TEACHING

If your perspective of American education is based on your experience as a student or that of a concerned citizen, this postulate will be barely visible, yet it is a driving force in shaping the education system. This motivates a large percentage of professional educators who in turn influence what and how things will be done in the school systems. The public's ignorance of this postulate drives up the cost of education and often lowers the quality of the system. It also makes a lie out of most school's published teacher-student ratio.

The city school that I worked for had 25,000 employees the year that I retired. Of these, only 10,600 were classroom teachers. The other 15 000 were "support" staff. This number did not include food service or custodian service people. These services were contracted out to private companies. There were relatively few bus drivers due to the fact that middle and high school students were given passes for public busses, streetcars and subways. That meant that for every two teachers, there were three people who collected a good salary not teaching.[19] Many of these "support" people

---

19 Politicians always point to the salaries of teachers as the major reason that the school systems spend so much money. What would happen if schools were required to spend 60% of their salary budget on classroom teachers rather than on "support" staff? No one wants to talk about this.

were certified teachers who moved out of the classroom into jobs that may or may not have been needed to operate the school system. There also were many teachers who only taught a class or two per day and were excused from teaching more classes to fulfill other duties.

—

One of the first things that a young teacher hears from some more experienced teachers is "if you're smart, you will find a way out of teaching classes." For a person who just spent many years of college, a pile of money preparing for a teaching career and the aggravation of getting the proper credentials and certificates to practice this profession in a geographical area, this does not make much sense. Yet this is one of the first pieces of advice that a beginning teacher is likely to receive. At first it may seem to be sour grapes from some teacher who is suffering from teacher burnout. It appears on the surface to be an invitation to change professions. Upon closer inspection one discovers that this is an incorrect interpretation of the advice.

One can be a "teacher" and collect the salary and benefits of being a teacher without really doing much or any actual teaching. It is all in understanding the system. Most middle and high school teachers are supposed to teach five or more classes a day. College teachers are usually expected to teach from nine to twelve credit hours or "contact" hours per week. But there are many different jobs that teachers do within the school that "relieves" them of some or most of their class teaching load. These positions free them from having to face classrooms full of students.

—

One of the first ways this can be done is by getting on committees (and how could any school possibly operate without committees, but that is another chapter) that must meet a half a day every week. This may seem easy but it is possibly the most painful way of ducking out of teaching all day every day. It does allow a teacher to catch up on all the gossip of the school and to learn who the movers and shakers are in this school. It has the disadvantage of being a transitory position. Every year the principal appoints new people to committees, re-appoints those who please him or her, and dissolves some committees and forms new committees to address current issues or problems. The advantage of being on committees for a young teacher or a teacher new to the school district is that you can get a better perspective of how the school operates and the methods and priorities of the principal. This knowledge allows you to avoid problems and take advantage of opportunities to make your job more enjoyable.

The next level of getting out of teaching a full load is by taking "extra" responsibilities such as being class sponsor. This type of job is usually good to reduce the teaching load by a period per day. These jobs tend to be more secure once you get the job. The trick is getting the job. Every school has its own list of "released from teaching" jobs that are available to teachers as an alternative to actually teaching students. Some schools have a position of publicity director, auditorium programs director, stage manager, audio-visual storage room manager, etc. The list is endless and varies with the district, principal, current trends in education, and phase of the moon when the school board approved the annual budget.

The trick is getting one of these jobs. It takes skill, timing and knowledge of the school politics. Keeping the position is relatively easy if you don't go out of your way to offend people.

Some of these "released from teaching" positions are controlled by certain academic departments. The department chairperson looks upon these positions as part of the department curriculum. For instance, the school newspaper and yearbook are often considered part of the exclusive domain of the English department.

It may be of benefit to relate the tale of how not to go about trying to get a "released from teaching" position. A school is a political institution and as such it follows unwritten rules that one must obey or be punished.

In one school the person teaching photography applied to be the year-book sponsor since the yearbook is mostly photographs. It seemed logical that a photographer would be able to do a good job. The English department chair went into a rage at the threat to his turf. His rebut to this affront went something like this:

"What kind of school would allow a non-English teacher to be year-book sponsor?"

(Aren't all teachers able to communicate and write clearly in the English language? This is only true when the students are found to be deficient in language skills and the English department wants to avoid being singled out)

All literary publications are part of the language department. (Who said that this must be so-the English chairman? This also is the operational definition of a racket.)

It's never been done this way before![20] (Conservatives are liberals who have obtained a position of power.)

The photography teacher violated Farber's first postulate and presented a logical case for his appointment to the position of yearbook sponsor. He counted the number of photographs and compared it to the number of complete sentences in the most recent yearbook. He reasoned that there was very little English language communication in the book and so it did little in giving students any writing experience. The large number of photographs that had to be taken, developed, printed, and cropped would extend to education of those students interested in photography and visual communication.

The photography teacher sealed his fate. He was doomed. There was no way that he would ever get out of the teaching a full load. Not only had he made an enemy of everyone in the English department but his logical and

---

20 This is one of the two arguments that almost always wins the case. The other argument is that "we did it once before and it was changed." (No one remembers why it was changed but there must have been a good reason.)

well researched argument made him a threat to the system. He was lucky that he was not scheduled to have 33 students in the darkroom at a time. The only thing that saved him from this fate was that the darkroom was only twelve by fifteen feet.

—

Even when a position is not controlled by a particular academic department, it is always possible for the situation to change.

In one school the faculty sponsor of the school newspaper was not a member of the English department. No one in the English department really wanted the position since the paper was being published weekly and this is a lot of work and a hard act to follow. The faculty sponsor held the position for over ten years and felt quite secure in the job. The school paper had a good reputation. The student newspaper staff was large and well organized. Things were going well.

Then a student article appeared that was critical of the English department. The student had been invited to report on an English department staff meeting. The report was less than flattering to certain members of the department. At this point the chairman of the English department decided that he wanted someone that he could control to be the sponsor of the student paper.

He first tried to "fire" the sponsor but found out that the sponsor was appointed by the head of the school. He then discovered that the budget for all publications was an adjunct to the English budget so he cut all funding for the school paper.

Ironically, there was no one in the English department who wanted the job of newspaper sponsor. That was not a problem for the chairman. He vowed that he would continue to withhold funding until he was given veto power over the appointment of the sponsor.

This saga could have been concluded several different ways but in this case the school was in the process of installing a new administration. In this situation, the new administration usually needs the support of the department chairs to get off on the right foot. The English chair prevailed.

Some academic departments seem more adapt at creating jobs that allow their teachers not to have to teach. In one school there were 14 teachers in the social studies department and not a one of these teachers taught a full teaching load. They had perfected the art of working themselves into various positions or creating positions that excused them from teaching duties. They had positions such as community relations director, adult education coordinator, class sponsor, community service director, student co-op work coordinator etc. One had to admire their ingenuity. Not only did they managed to get into "released from teaching" positions but in several cases were actually receiving additional pay for doing less teaching.

The laws of supply and demand can have an effect on the ability of members of a particular academic department to receive non-teaching teaching positions. There has always been a surplus of history teachers so that a school or principal has no trouble hiring teachers in this area. If fact, many private schools will not consider a person for a job in their social studies department unless the person is capable of and agrees to coach a major sport. These schools usually do not pay coaches much and in many private schools every instructor is *required* to supervise some extracurricular activity. Public schools usually have paid coaches but they are usually not very well compensated except for the football coaches. It is best to have a sports background if you are studying to be a social studies, English, or art teacher.

The opposite is often true of math and science teachers. The supply is usually limited since many of these people can easily go into industry and business positions. There was a time when the average science teacher taught for less than ten years before leaving teaching for the better paying jobs of business and industry. School administrators are reluctant to allow these teachers out of the classroom because it is too difficult to find good replacements.

There is one way that teachers in these areas often use to get out of teaching classes. School administrators are still afraid of computers. They need someone to program and operate the school's computers. Many principals look at science and math teachers as "nerds" and believe that they can run the computers better than anyone else. Most of us know that we no longer need to write computer programs any more, we just buy and install the software that is needed for the particular task. This means that science and math teachers usually are not any better than a social studies teacher when it comes to running the school's computer system. Please keep this a secret.

—

One of the more interesting "released from teaching" positions is that of "museum teacher." In the larger cities teachers have created teaching jobs that don't even require them to report to a school. Instead they are assigned to a public museum to be the on-site expert to schedule, coordinate, or be the tour guide for school field trips to that facility. There are teachers assigned to the zoo, courthouse, nature centers, art museums, historical sites, science or technical museums, etc. This is a way that a city can support and staff these museums indirectly. It also relieves the museum experts of the problems of giving tours to students whose main interest in visiting is to get a day out of classroom (they must have learned from their teachers). The museum teacher does not have the responsibility of controlling the behavior of students; that is the visiting classroom teacher's duty. Some days there may be few or no tours-especially Friday afternoons. This can evolve into an easy job since the museum teacher usually needs only to prepare one good tour lesson, and then can teach and refine the same lesson every day for the school year. One year, our district's "best teacher of the year" was a museum teacher. The irony of this is not lost on the regular classroom teachers who prepared several different lessons for every day of the 180 plus days of the school year. The teacher who prepared the fewest lessons and teaches the least is the *most successful teacher.* This teacher got the public recognition and praise while the "real" teachers are more likely to be recipients of "teacher bashing" in the local newspaper or by the tax payers association. They will be called lazy and overpaid every year when the annual school budget comes up for a vote or when it is time to negotiate a new teachers' contract.

—

One of the most seemingly unlikely paths to get one of these "released from teaching" teaching positions is to be a tenured teacher who is a royal pain in the butt to the principal. There are many principals who use their power to give out and take away these "released from teaching" jobs as a way of controlling "problem" teachers. Any teacher who is elected to a leadership position in the teachers' union seems suddenly have some sort of job that allows them not to have to spend much time in a classroom.[21] Sometimes it is the teacher who speaks out too often or complains too much in faculty meetings who is suddenly the coordinator of something or other. These people learn quickly not to bite the hand that fed them this non-teaching teacher job. They don't speak out in meetings any more unless it is to criticize the classroom teachers for not doing enough. They certainly don't disagree with the principal, his ideas, or policies.

Sometimes the complainers are "promoted" to a purely administrative position. This can be the first step on the route to becoming a school principal.

In the better schools the administration appointments are made based on the Peter Principle.[22] In many other schools administrative positions

---

21 This also serves to separate teacher union representatives from the classroom teacher. This causes the classroom teachers to grow distrustful of their elected leaders and thus weakens the teachers' organization. A successful principal learns to keep the teachers divided, thereby maximizing his/her control.

22 Dr. Lawrence Peter first described the principle that is evident in many organizations. Simply stated, a person will continue to be promoted until finally promoted to one level beyond their competence. They will continue in this position for which they are incompetent to the distraction of all who must work with them. Dr. Peter was a teacher.

are filled as a means of controlling the loudest complainers. In many cases these are teachers who are unable to be effective in the classroom and their complaints are a smoke screen to hide their incompetence. In other cases it is a matter of whether the present administrators (to quote President Lyndon Johnson, a former school teacher) want "the camel pissing into the tent or out of the tent." Thus in school systems a person can rise several levels above their level of incompetence. The principle described and named by Dr. Peter does not apply in education because it is too logical. In some school systems people are promoted until they quit complaining. Often they only quit when they are in an extremely insecure position due to the fact they have been promoted *several* levels beyond their competence.

—

There are several other avenues to non-teaching teaching positions. One of the most used is to become a "counselor." This is one of the first things that young teachers should consider if they can't or don't want to handle the problems of teaching. Counselors only see students that the counselor chooses to see. They never need to see more than one or two students at a time. They never have to face an entire classroom of students alone. If they choose to enter a classroom, the regular teacher is often required to stay in the room. It requires graduate level courses to get an additional certificate. Universities find no trouble filling classrooms with people who want a counseling certificate. This is because once a person is appointed to a counseling position, they are set for life. It is only under the most unusual circumstances that a counselor will be forced back into the classroom.

Becoming a counselor takes time and money. It can take years to get in all the necessary courses in night school. One must pay for tuition, transportation, and books. In some schools this is partly refunded by the school system. Other times the only recovery of any these cost is that they are deductible on your income tax. Since counseling in open to anyone who is willing to spend the time and money. The counseling field and opportunities are expanding by leaps and bounds. Counselors must be ranked as some of the most successful non-teaching teachers.

—

An easier path to a "released from teaching" position is that of roster office. In most schools there must be one or more full time persons to schedule the students into the correct classes. This is a more complex task in middle and high schools where not all the students are taking the same level and subjects as their peers.

In theory, the principal is responsible for the master schedule of the school. Then an assistant has the task of developing the schedules for the individual students. The master schedule is put on computer. The student's subject selection is then entered and the computer sorts though the schedule of course offerings and times and prints out a "best fit" schedule for the student.

In reality, the principals are appointed primary for their ability to handle public relations. While he or she is supposed to have an understanding of bookkeeping, accounting and scheduling, the actual work will be assigned to others. The principal knows what courses the school needs to offer the students. This is set by the state and expanded by the school board and the curriculum committee within the school. He/she needs the counselors or someone to gather information on how many sections of each subject will be needed next year. This changes from year to year with changing student numbers and interests and teacher availability. Then he/she needs to know which teachers are qualified to teach each subject. Teacher certification and teacher contract limitations have made this more complex. Many middle school principals now want all the faculty in this type of a school to be certified as elementary teachers since they can be assigned to teach any subject. High school certification limits the subjects that a teacher can be assigned to teach. The department heads and subject chairpersons gather this information. (Someone has to collect and correlate this data.)

Thus the roster office is born. A math or computer teacher is released from teaching to run this operation. Since all of this work is by nature seasonal, there are certain times of the school year that there is a lot of work to be done. The counselors have other work to do and are not available for this. However, the counselor is the only one who can determine what classes a student should take but then it is the problem of the roster office to figure out how to schedule the student into all of those subjects. Soon there are several teachers "released from teaching" to use the computer to get the students scheduled into the correct classes.

The teachers in the roster office work very hard at the beginning and the end of each school year. In between, there should not be very much work. This could lead to problems for them if the administration discovered that they were not doing anything. The trick here is to have either work in a school with a large transient population or have enough errors in student or teacher schedules to keep busy with these individual scheduling problems. In many city schools, there are more than a hundred students transferred in and out of a school every month. Each of these students must be scheduled into new classes. Students leaving the school must be dropped from classes to make room for the incoming transfers.

Often no one gets around to looking at summer school transcripts until a student complains that they are in a course that they have already completed in summer school. At this point the roster office must rearrange the student's class schedule to get him or her in the correct classes. Often the need to change one course means that all the student's classes be changed in order to find openings in other courses that fit the student's course selections. The students transferred from a class are called "drops." The students transferred into a class are called "adds." I have been in schools where it was "normal" to have 165 students assigned to your classes on the first day of school and then have 200 student "drops" and "adds" by the end of the school term.

The teachers in the roster office are successful teachers. This is a job very few administrators could or would do, so the teachers in the roster jobs are immune to being forced to teach as long as the student rosters appear on time and without too many conflicts.[23] Since the roster office has the power to give individual teachers easy or difficult schedules, the teachers learn not to complain about the "work" done by the teachers in this office.

—

Another avenue open to teachers to be "released from teaching" is the position of department chairperson or department head. The difference in these positions vary from school to school but generally a chairperson is "released from teaching" while a department head may be both "released from teaching" and given an increase in salary. Once a person is appointed to one of these positions it is unusual for them to lose it.

The stated responsibilities of these positions usually include the requisition of supplies and matching the teachers with the courses within the department. The real responsibility of the chairman is to referee disputes between students and teachers or worse, parents and teachers. The chairperson or department head is usually required to teach at least one class of his/her choice. This usually results in the department head teaching an advanced elective class. This is usually a rather small class of straight A students. These students are the type that would do well no matter whether they have a good or bad teacher. This becomes a model class that functions like a seminar. The department chairperson does not have to teach much and therefore has become the most successful teacher in the department. The school administrators and parents alike believe that the department head is the best teacher in the department. The success of these A students

---

23   It is hard to know how many student schedule conflicts are too many. Some really successful roster offices can get away with very large numbers if they can blame them on the counselors and then correct them over a period of several months.

selected for this class is proof of good teaching.

The chairperson or department head usually has some responsibility for development of curriculum and the selection of textbooks. Once this is in place it is a rather simple matter to continue it year after year with minor adjustments to keep it current. In most school districts curriculum continues to evolve as the teachers see what works with their students. It is seldom that a school makes a major overall change in curriculum. Most major curriculum changes are developed by universities with state or federal grant money. Then the university, with help from a publisher, will try to convince school districts to adopt the newly developed curriculum.

A successful chairman will take time off from being in school every year to go to workshops and conventions to keep up with all the new curriculum developments. The travel, lodging and meals are usually covered by the school district. A successful chairman will always be "studying" possible curriculum changes without actually implementing them. This is due to the fact that major curriculum changes require a lot of work and are risky. They may not work out as well as the present curriculum so it is better not to change. A chairperson who has an eye on a promotion is more likely to institute curriculum change. With luck, the chairman will be promoted before the full long range effects of the curriculum change can be determined.

—

It used to be that if a teacher can change light bulbs in overhead projectors and dust the lenses of film projectors, then they were often qualified to be the A-V coordinator. In most states this does not yet require a master's degree in A-V or media systems. The more progressive states were requiring a certificate in this field. In many smaller schools this is a *released from teaching* position where the person may only be required to teach as little as one class per day and to be available to handout and collect projectors, tape recorders, VCRs, etc. for the remainder of the school day. This often avoids the need for special certification or degrees.

This person can occupy this/her spare time looking through catalogues of light bulbs, educational films, video tapes etc. They can organize, label, and catalogue all the various records, audio and video tapes, films DVDs, etc. that are already in the school. A good A-V coordinator should be able to get the teachers to use more and more of the equipment and thus increase the amount of time that the A-V coordinator needs to be available rather than teaching. A good A-V person can go from teaching one *less* period per day to *only* teaching one period per day in just a couple of years. Of course he or she may have to spend some time at a local university taking courses to become a certified A-V or *media* specialist if the job becomes a full time non-teaching teaching job. Care must be exercised not to expand the job faster that you can obtain the credentials in this area.

This position is now being converted to an IT specialist position. This person installs software on the school computers, maintains a library of computer software and continuously removes virus from school computers. The school needs someone to keep its servers up, maintain passwords and generally keep track of the school computers. As schools and teachers become more dependent on computers, this position becomes more powerful. Since most school districts will not pay the salary demanded by highly trained IT people, the teacher willing and able to do this for a lowly teacher's salary can negotiate a very comfortable teaching load. This office is often also charged with checking school computers for unlicensed software. This is a real problem in most schools.

—

Another path to a being a teacher who does not teach is to get an advanced degree. Most teachers are required to complete a master's degree to obtain a "permanent" teaching certificate. The majority of teachers do not earn a degree beyond this level but may continue to do more course work to become certified in different areas. A few teachers enroll in doctorate program.

I was rather ignorant of why people earned doctorates when I enrolled in a doctorate program. I wanted to be a top teacher. The last phase of the program is to prepare a dissertation proposal. As I entered this phase of the program my advisor kept asking me what I planned to do when I finished the degree. The dissertation subject is the phase that makes a person an "expert" in something. The choice of a topic should be based on the next professional direction that the person wants to pursue. I told him that I planned to do the same things that I was presently doing (teaching 5 periods of high school science per day), at first he didn't believe me. Then he thought that something was wrong with me. Did I lack ambition? Why was I even working on this degree if I was *only* going to teach students?

A couple of months after this conversation my advisor and everyone on my doctorate dissertation committee were given layoff notices by the university. Although they were all tenured professors, the university was having some financial difficulty and decided to cut staff and programs. Ironically all the courses and classes in science and math education were full. The enrollment of the master's degree programs in these departments was growing. Although there was a need for more math and science teachers, the university staff of these profitable departments were cut in half. There were no cuts in the staff of the department of Educational Administration even though their classes were not full. It was obvious to many of us that the purpose of the graduate school of education was not to produce better classroom teachers. It was to provide programs to allow teachers to *move out of the classroom.* The courses offered in the math and science educational departments were designed to promote better teaching of math and science in the classroom.

The sad truth of the matter is that people earn doctorates in education not to be better teachers but as a way to get out of classroom teaching. A person with a doctorate who is still a classroom teacher is considered a failure my most of his or her peers. People who hold doctorates are considered successful only when they are supervisors, coordinators, curriculum planners, program directors, authors, textbook editors etc. They almost never *teach* below college level for very long after earning such a degree.

—

There are a few teachers who must be really crazy or just plain stupid. They will take on what I think is the worst, most depressing job in any school just to get out of the classroom. These teachers apply for and get non-teaching teaching jobs as "deans." The dean's office handles the most difficult student discipline cases. They get the fun job of dealing with the students that the teacher and department head could not handle. They get to handle fights in and around the school. They get criticized by most of the other teachers for the way they handle one case or another. There is no way that they can please all of the staff. They can displease one hundred percent of the teachers in many cases because school policy or school law or outside pressures severely limits their options in many cases. The deans serve in these positions at the pleasure of the building principal and can be returned to the classroom anytime they displease the powers that be. These teachers have to be really desperate to get out of teaching.

The deans have the power to punish students, suspend students, refer students to outside agencies (social agencies, police, etc.), and recommend students to be expelled from school. Because students perceive the deans as having a lot of clout, the students will listen carefully to a dean. A dean can become the most respected counselor in the building even though he or she is not a certified counselor.

There are people who enjoy the position of dean and spend many years in this position rather than teach in a classroom. In other cases this position is looked upon or used as a stepping stone to an appointed administrative position such as vice principal. It is a needed and useful position within a school but not one I would recommend to you. It takes a special type of person to work in this job and retain ones sanity.

—

There are many teachers who hold an administrative certificate and would jump at the opportunity to get a job as a vice principal or principal. Education is one of the few occupations where most of the leadership is almost entirely from promotion up from the ranks. This has its good points and its bad points.

The good point is that every principal has had the experience of running a classroom and should be able to relate to the situation of the teacher.

The other side is that the experience gained in running a classroom does not prepare a person for administrating a school in the complex world of today. Most experienced teachers can give examples of outstanding teachers who were very poor principals and of very poor teachers who became outstanding principals. This means that it is not possible to reliably predict which teacher will be the best administrator. Administration is an entirely different occupation from teaching. This is no different from other occupations. In business and industry, accountants, engineers, and others are "promoted" out of their area of expertise into administrative jobs. The only difference is that teachers must go back to school and earn an administrative certificate before they can be considered for an administrative position.

In most school districts, the process of selecting administrators is rather political. Some larger school districts have a written screening test based on knowledge of the current trends and jargon in education, recent school law and the policies of the district. This simply narrows the field before the politics of the school district or board come into play. The result of this is that the path to such a position is uncertain and not for everyone.

Although there are better ways of getting a non-teaching teaching job, the administrative positions usually pay more. If school boards were more astute about the laws of supply and demand, they would find that they could pay principals *less* than classroom teachers and they would still not have difficulty filling the jobs with certified (and qualified) people. There are many teachers who would take a pay cut to get out of the classroom, especially if they were moving to a position of authority and status in the community.

—

At one school where I was teaching, the principal received an award for being an outstanding principal. He decided that the reason that he got the award was that his school had an outstanding staff and that they should share in the benefits. He took the money from the prize and established a fund to provide a plaque and a check for one outstanding *teacher* every year.

This principal's good intentions backfired. It ended up dividing the staff and created some hard feelings. The principal should have stated that the award was for outstanding "teaching" since teaching is the primary function of the school but he didn't. When he realized his mistake, it was too late to change it.

First there had to be a committee to establish the method of selection of the school's outstanding teachers of the year. Normally very few people want to serve on such a committee because it is a no win situation. Everyone who did not get picked for the prize is disappointed and you only get into trouble when you try to explain to someone why they were not selected.

This year was different. The school district had selected someone as the outstanding teacher of the district who did not teach but ran a weekly seminar type session of a dozen or so selected students. The "regular" teachers were fuming. They decided (me included) that it was time to get involved. There were more volunteers for the committee than expected. There had to be some way to reduce the number. This was done by limiting the number from each department so that there would be a "balance."

At the first committee meeting it was proposed that the award be given only to someone who taught a full teaching load. The feeling was that these people who are in the classroom all day should be recognized. However there were several non-teaching teachers on the committee. They strenuously objected to this proposal. One person who had a non-teaching teaching job said that *if they were not an outstanding teacher, they would be still teaching five classes per day.* This was a telling but a sad commentary on the status of the classroom teacher. We can easily overlook such a comment made by someone outside of education, however, *we in the teaching profession, are sometimes our worst enemies.*

Most of the non-teaching teaching jobs in any school provide a needed part of the educational program. Many of the teachers in these positions work harder than they would work in the classroom while others may take advantage. That is human nature. Contrary to the opinion of some people, having a non-teaching teacher position is not an indication that the person was a good teacher (unless you believe in the Peter Principle). Teachers in non-teaching positions usually have more contact with parents and the public in general. This may be why the public gives them more respect than the classroom teacher.

Unfortunately this is a concept that we in the classroom must live with. Both the public and some members of our profession seem to believe that successful teachers are those who do not teach. You don't have to agree with the public's definition. *You have to define success for yourself* but don't expect to change the perception of others. There are many of us, in fact most of us, that are proud of our successes in the classroom and don't need to fit the public perception of a successful educator to feel that we are successful in education.

In Robert Bolt's *A Man for All Seasons,* a young Cambridge scholar named Richard Rich approaches Sir Thomas More for advice on the choice of a career. Rich is ambitious and anxious to rise in the world.

More suggests, "Why not be a teacher? You'd be a fine teacher. Perhaps even a great one."

Rich contemptuously retorts, "And if I was, who would know it?"

More replied, "You, your pupils, your friends, God. Not a bad public, that …"

CHAPTER 6

Farber's Sixth Postulate

LE CHATELIER'S PRINCIPLE APPLIES IN EDUCATION AS WELL AS CHEMISTRY

Le Chatelier's principle is a principle that you probably have either never heard of or quickly forgot. This is because it is only found in chemistry books. Chemists believe that it is a principle of chemistry alone and they don't want to share it with non-chemists. This is very selfish of them since it applies more to American education establishment that to the world of chemistry. It states that if there exists a state of chemical equilibrium in a closed system and then stress or change is imposed on this system, the equilibrium will shift to counteract the change or stress.

A very wise man once told me that *there is only one thing that never changes, human nature.* The educational system is made up of people who will respond in predictable ways to most changes. *They will resist them.* It seems to be a part of human nature. For many people there is a security in doing things the same way day after day and year after year even when the results are not satisfactory. There is a risk in change. The majority of people do not wish to take any risk that is avoidable. When changes are forced upon people they will make changes is their life style, work habits and methods that tend to counteract the change imposed on them.

The lack of true understanding of this postulate may result in people trying to correct problems only to find that their solutions are not effective for very long. This leads to a system of "management by drives." Everyone has experienced this type of management at one time or another. In schools it tends to take different forms depending on the seasons and academic schedule. In football season, it is school spirit. Later the drive is to get students to class on time Then it is keeping our school clean, in spring it is proper dress for school. The lists of drives are without end but each lasts about four to six weeks and then another drive is instituted. People are very good at catching on to the cycles and quickly adapt to them. One method that is used to counteract a drive is to generate a lot of paper work. People write directives, create new forms (to be filled out by others, of course) and generally clog up the normal flow of communications. Some people devise methods of creating more paperwork for the person or group which initiated the drive, thus making sure that the drive is not expanded and is short lived. Other people learn to give lip service to the drive at the beginning and then just ignore it altogether within a month. These people know that the drive will be over in a short while.

In education on a state or national level, the cycles or drives will last much longer but experienced educators know that the drive will not last and are alert for signs that it is on the wane. On a school district level the cycle will average about two or three years. Most school boards and superintendents don't last more than five years. The first few years the "new" superintendent devises a plan to improve the school system in some way. In a while the great plan wanes as there is no sustained improvement in standardized test scores and the superintendent begins to send out resumes or give speeches in other towns or states. The teachers and building principals are usually in for the long haul and know that they will still be in the school long after the current board or superintendent are just old memories.

So how does this Le Chatelier's principle apply to education in general? The educational system in this country is much like a closed system. The state department of educational issues teaching certificates. The state requires the prospective teachers to take a specific group of courses. The course requirements are different for elementary and secondary teachers. In addition secondary teachers are required to take specific courses in each subject that they wish to teach. Once the prospective teacher has completed the required courses, a few elective courses, student teaching and an undergraduate degree, they are issued a *provisional* teaching certificate. This permits them to teach in a public school for only a few years. To obtain a *permanent* certificate, the person must take a series of graduate level courses. Many states require a master's degree or the equivalent for a permanent certificate. Some states now require all teachers to take a specific number of graduate courses every five years also to continue to teaching in public schools. Of course, all of these courses are taught by the state colleges. By state law, public school boards can only hire state certified teachers and administrators. Children under a specific age are required to attend school. This is a closed loop.[24] In other words, it is a closed system. It therefore, Le Chatelier's principle is applicable.

The most interesting part of this closed state controlled system is that every few years' politicians make an issue of the preparation of teachers. They make speeches to the effect that the teachers are not properly prepared to teach. The public never remembers that these very same politicians control the course requirements for a teaching certificate. Most teachers would not willing pay to take many of the "methods" courses offered by the colleges of education rather they are forced to do so by the state. The state mandated the course requirements for teachers and, like most bureaucracy, it grows like a cancer. Teachers have to take not only method courses in each subject, they must take courses in the history of education, the organization of schools, how to do a bulletin board, psychology, test writing, and special education. Most of these are completely useless for the classroom teacher, but, by requiring these courses, the state effectively prevents the teacher from taking more courses in their specific subject area. To teach physics for example, a person is now required to take two semesters of special education. Which would be better, another physics or math course or the special education course? The teacher has no

---

24   If this were not operated by the state, it would fit the definition of a racket.

choice. The state teacher colleges and the state departments of education will work together to fill the classrooms of colleges of education. It has little or nothing to do with developing better teachers. This follows Farber's first postulate and is supported by Farber's seventh postulate.[25]

My first graduate level course after a year of teaching was entitled "teaching reading in the high school." This was an evening class and the classroom was filled with young high school teachers. The instructor began by talking about reading scores of high school students and discussing that there was a need to teach reading in high school. This went on for a couple of weeks at which time the teachers in class asked the professor when he was going to instruct us on how to help our students improve their reading skills. The reply was that the scope of this course is *only to define* the scope of reading problems in high schools. If we wanted to know how to help improve reading in the high school, we would have to take the next level course which, of course, we would not be permitted to take until we successfully completed this course. The teachers wasted two evenings per week, study time, and the cost of tuition, books, and transportation to listen to a professor talk about a problem that they faced every day and gained nothing in the way of methods, materials, or information that would help their students improve reading skills. Yes, this was a required course for a permanent certificate. The higher level (and possibly useful) course was an elective.

Part of being a true professional is self-regulation. Other professions have a system which is just as closed and they have even more control over the regulation of their field. The legal profession, for instance, is even more of a closed system since they control the courts and much of the legislature. The public has much more influence over education since the majority of

---

25   "Education theory and practice is not based on science, it's based on economics." There are many theories to support the course requirements for a teaching certificate, but survey any group of veteran teachers and they will tell you that these courses were a waste of their time and money.

elected school boards are made up of people who are usually not educators. In some states, educators are prohibited by law from serving on a school board. Imagine what would happen if the majority of legislators and/or Supreme Court judges were not permitted to be members of the legal profession.

Unfortunately, teachers and their organizations will work to maintain rather than change the system. Teachers are their own worst enemy. The certification system limits the teaching profession to those who are dedicated enough to put up with these requirements and sit through these dull courses. The unions see certification as a way of limiting the supply of teachers.[26] Unions believe that the law of supply and demand will increase teachers' salaries.[27] Teachers have learned that they can earn a higher salary if they earn more graduate credits or have multiple types of teaching certificates. In many school districts, the school will pay part or all of the tuition for continuing education for tenured teachers. This means that in some cases, the school district pays the tuition for a teacher to take courses so that the district can then pay the same teacher a higher salary.

Stresses or pressures can be exerted from the outside of the system in education the same as we can change things in a chemical equilibrium even they may exist in a closed flask or test tube. The pressure, temperature and other things can be changed chemical system contained in a closed flask. In a chemical system the atoms and molecules rearrange themselves, if possible, in such a way as to relieve the pressure or stress. The actual number, mass and types of atoms can not be changed in a closed system. They can

---

26 All professional organizations will use the government to limit the supply. Back in the 1990s the government required medical schools to reduce the number of admissions in order to continue their government grants. This was in the name of improving healthcare.

27 The state can quickly change or even drop the certificate requirements, thus controlling the supply and cost of certified teachers. In many states, people do not have to be certified to teach in charter schools and private schools.

only be rearranged. When the pressure from the outside is removed, the atoms will reform the arrangement in which they existed before the pressure was applied.

The people in education do respond in the same way to pressures or stresses on their system or school. An outside pressure or stress will cause them to change in some way to relieve the pressure or stress, but when the outside pressure or stress is removed, they will revert to doing things in the way they did them before the stress was applied. It is unusual to have a pressure applied long enough in education that the change or shift that it induces has a lasting effect. This usually takes another generation of educators.

It is a truism that most teachers teach in the same way that they were taught. This is fact, not a judgment or criticism. If the teacher was able to learn by a particular teaching method, then it is natural that the teacher would expect his or her students to be able to learn by the same method. Many people would argue that it would be a disservice to the students to try something new when there is already an old method that worked for the previous generation. If it works, don't fix it. The fix may cause it not to work at all. Teachers ask themselves whether it is worth the risk. Should they take a chance on something that may not work with their students and cause these students to be deficient in some way? Teachers are usually willing to try new methods only when their students are trying and not successful in learning in the present situation.

Notice the catch clause "… *students are trying.*" Teachers are not going to fault the teaching method unless they are convinced that the students are making an honest effort to learn. If students are trying and not succeeding, then and only then are teachers willing to adopt a new method. As long as teachers believe that the reason for poor grades is the lack of effort on the part of the student, the school is not to blame. This is usually the first reason we use against changing the way we run our schools and classes. Schools have been operated more or less the same way for most of the last century and most of the students somehow got through the schools. These students are now the adults who today are running the businesses, industries, and schools.

Teachers must instruct groups of students, not individuals. Therefore the teacher feels obligated to teach in a method that is successful for the majority of the group. An individual student who is trying and cannot learn in this situation creates a dilemma for the teacher and / or the school ... Does the teacher change the teaching to better suit this individual and risk losing the progress and success of the group? Ideally the teacher should have time to give this student special attention. This is not usually the case. Another solution is to move the individual to another group. Does the school provide a different type of instruction that is better suited to this student's learning style? If the student is determined to be in a "special educational" classification, then there may be solution within the school system. If the student does not fit into this category, then it is usually the student who will have to make some accommodation.

—

In a chemical equilibrium system, the equilibrium is usually not stationary. Most chemical equilibria are dynamic. That means that the system is constantly changing, but the forward direction and speed of the change is equal to the backward direction and speed of the change. An easy way to visualize this is to think of a river. If you were to visit the same location along a river bank, you would see a river that may look the same for several days in a row. In fact each day you would be seeing a different river. All the water that you saw the first day has moved downstream out of your sight. The water in this river has been changed and yet the river looks the same. The amount of water that flowed from upstream was equal to the amount of water that flowed downstream. The volume or weight of water that was changed may have been tremendous. Think about if you had to move that much water by human devices. It would be a major undertaking requiring much effort or engineering skill ... Yet, the result of all of this change was no change. This is what is meant by the term "dynamic equilibrium."

Schools are much the same as the river. Every year new students enter the school replacing the older students who graduated, transferred, or dropped out. The average age, size, etc. of the student body does not significantly change over time. Each generation of students have the same problems although each generation believes that their problems are unique. Each generation has its distinctive dress, new jargon, and music with a distinctive primitive beat. Each generation of students present the same set of problems for the school. One of the functions of the school is to control and contain the students until they mature, find some direction, and outgrow their problems.

There are some people who try to correct problems by making alterations to policies, systems and schedules. These changes often do not take into account that human nature does not change nor do they understand Le Chatelier's principle. The result is that the effect of the alterations is often short lived. People quickly make counter adjustments that negate the intended change.

One school had a problem with late students. The teachers were complaining to the principal about students being late to first period class. The principal did a survey of the lateness and found that there were about two hundred and fifty to three hundred students (one tenth of the student population) who were late every day. Most of these students were not more than fifteen minutes late for school. He came up with a simple and logical solution to the problem. He changed the school schedule by fifteen minutes. The late bell was fifteen minutes later in the morning and the dismissal bell was fifteen minutes later in the afternoon. He thought that he had found the perfectly logical solution. This change was designed to avoid the problems associated with having the school administration establish penalties to deter lateness. This is never popular with students and parents.

The first week of the new schedule the solution appeared to work. By the second week of the new schedule there was a definite increase in lateness. By the third week there were as many students late to school as there had been before the schedule changes. This logical change was in violation of Farber's first postulate and Farber's sixth postulate would have forecast what was going to occur.

This is a typical example of Le Chatelier's principle. People in a school, as a group, usually reach a dynamic equilibrium. The people at this school, staff and students alike had adjusted their alarm clocks and morning routines by fifteen minutes. The same percentage of people who over slept or did not allow adequate time to get to school on time before the change did the same thing after the change. The sum total of all the changes was no change.

—

One of the problems that is most often discussed in the relationship to schools is the academic standards. This is a problem that will be discussed in more detail in the eleventh chapter: *Education is the only business where the customer is satisfied with less and less product.* The human brain is believed to be the result of the expression of the chromosomes just like every other part of the human body. The brain, like a muscle, can only be developed to an extent that is determined by its chromosomal design. It has its limitations. A child can not be expected to lift a three hundred pound weight. Likewise a child can not be expected to understand the principles of nuclear physics.

Part of the every teacher's job is to determine if a student learned enough to be successful in the study of more complex subjects. The teacher must report how much each student has learned in his or her class.

Grading is also called *sorting*. The basic objective of any grading system is to sort some similar objects according to some observable characteristic. We sort or grade everything from eggs to diamonds. People fail to appreciate that this is what the school or teacher is required to do with students by colleges, business and industry. These other institutions are the consumers of the schools' product and want to be able to select the product that best fits their needs. Different grades of diamonds have different uses.

Some are used in jewelry, some as drill bits, and others as bearings. The same can be said of eggs.

Politicians and school superintendents are always looking for a way of grading that please the current trend. Sometimes it is raising education standards, other times it is to tell every parent that their child is gem. The truth is that the population of students doesn't really change. So changing grading systems can not really change the basic results, only confuse the parents and the schools' customers (i.e. business, industry, and colleges).

Years ago the grading system in most schools went something like this.

90–100%	A
80–89%	B
70–79%	C
60–69%	D
below 60%	F

Without repeating the discussion of what core of knowledge constitutes 100%, this was an accepted norm that most schools followed.

Then some school somewhere decided that they had to have higher academic standards. They wanted the world to know that a grade of C in their school was the equivalent of some of the B grades in other schools. They produced a grading system that looked like this.

93–100%	A
84–92%	B
75–83%	C
66–74%	D
65% and below	F

As soon as one school in an area changed its number value of the letter grades, all neighboring schools formed grade study committees. Hundreds and even thousands of man-hours were spent by every district to set new number standards for their letter grades. If the neighboring district had 66% as its lowest passing grade, the next district set its lowest passing grade as 70%.

College admissions offices were being driven nuts with school districts changing systems. Some school districts changed their system more than twice. Can you imagine what the grade explanation part of a student transcript must have looked like. A grade of B earned before 9/78 is 80–90%, earned between 9/78 and 9/79 is 82–92% and after 9/80 is 84–94% No wonder the colleges want to see the student's SAT scores before processing their application.

One grade study committee asked each teacher to comment in writing as to what he or she thought the number value for each letter grade should be. These letters were then to be read and discussed at the next faculty meeting. By this time I had enough of this foolishness so I proposed the following scale.

100%	A
99%	B
98%	C
97%	D
96% and below	F

I told the committee that this was the only logical thing to do and it would make them the highest academic district in the area. It would provide our school board and citizens of the district bragging rights over every other district in the state. The memo concluded that there would be no change in the number of students in each grade category because the numbers are meaningless without a precise definition of exactly what the core content, skills, or work required to have completed 100% of the specific course.

Of course my memo was ignored and after many hours of discussion the faculty and administration raised the numbers that each letter grade represented by a percentage point or two.

I was able to see the grades of the students of three different school districts during these changes and the percentage of students receiving A's, B's, C's, etc. in each subject did not change significantly. Teachers and school districts know that principals, parents, school board, and taxpayers will not tolerate a very high percentage of low letter grades. The teaching staff adjusted their grading procedures to accommodate the change in the grading scale so that there was no change. Did the students learn more? I don't think so. The SAT scores of the students in these districts did not change significantly. This is Le Chatelier's principle in education.

You may wonder how teachers adjusted their tests to meet the new higher numbers for passing. Some teachers gave students 10% for having their name or a heading on the test paper. Other teachers gave a number of "extra credit" questions on every test. One district that gave a district-wide final exam in each subject published an "official" conversion scale for its exams. A score of 60 correct answers out of a hundred questions was to be called 72%, 61 or 62 correct became a 73%, 63 or 64 correct became 74% and so on. People are very creative when it comes to ways to resist actual change.

Another superintendent of schools was concerned about the failure and dropout rate in the school system. This person tried to solve these problems by lowering the passing score by five percent. This change had no effect on the failure rate or dropout rate the next year. The teachers simply adjusted the way that they scored homework and tests to accommodate the changes imposed by the superintendent.

—

An understanding of Le Chatelier's principle may allow you to quickly determine the problems and guiding philosophy of a school. The leadership of the school (i.e. the school's principal) applies a constant pressure on the people in the school. If you can determine the background and areas of expertise of the leaders of the school, you can usually predict the true direction of that school or the major problems faced by the school. Principals are appointed either to solve an existing set of problems or to lead in a direction desired by the community or school board. Principals apply a constant pressure on the closed system of the school and their tenure is usually long enough that teachers accept the directions emphasized by the principal or they leave. The principal usually has a say on the hiring of teachers and would tend to favor teachers that seem to agree with his/her emphasis. This pressure over time will tend to shift the equilibrium of the school.

A principal who was formerly an English or language teacher will be more likely to pressure the teachers to assign more homework and be stricter on grading. School publications, drama, choir, band, and orchestra would have equal status with the athletic teams. This school would tend to be a more academic school. The headmasters of many private schools came from the ranks of language teachers and often emphasis the classics.

The school that has a former gym teacher or football coach as principal would tend to be a school that had or has some problems with student behavior. Remember that coaches do not necessarily have to be physical education teachers. Often a physical education teacher will be appointed as vice principal to handle student discipline problems and, upon the retirement of the principal, simply becomes the principal. This school usually places emphasis on community relations, school spirit, band, and general appearance of the physical plant. Teachers are not likely to be criticized for giving too many high grades, but may be questioned about failing grades especially why a member of an athletic team was not given a passing grade.

It is not unusual to find that the principal is a former math teacher or business teacher. This is a school that is watching its budget closely and wants leadership that can find ways to keep track of where the money is being spent. This person has to be able to communicate and justify the school budget to the school board's accountants. In this school the paperwork will flow smoothly and things will be organized in a timely fashion. The relative roles of the various departments of the school will reflect the strength and leadership ability of the department chairpersons or department heads.

There are some principals that came from the ranks of social studies teachers. These principals tend to operate the school by committee. They are more likely to ask the school department heads to propose school procedures, solutions to problems etc. As long as these advising groups can reach agreement about the direction that the school should take in various situations, the principal will continue following this administrative method.

I've only experienced two principals that were former science teachers. Science teachers who want to make more money or who are unhappy in the classroom are more likely to quit teaching and take a job in industry. They usually have more opportunity in industry than social studies, language, or physical education teachers. The same is true of industrial arts and vocational educational teachers.

While all of the above is an over simplification of judging a school's leadership, it is an example of how Le Chatelier's principle can be and often is applied to change the equilibrium of a school.

—

Most people believe that the direction and philosophy of education is much different from what it was years ago. Some people believe that schools no longer can prepare students for careers because the world is changing too quickly. They point to new fields that employ large numbers of people that didn't even exist two decades ago and point to shrinking opportunities in other areas where robots and computers have replaced large numbers of workers. They will say that schools must prepare students differently today and the objectives of the schools much be changed.

In 1918 the National Education Association Commission on the Reorganization of Secondary Education (CRSE) wrote *The Cardinal*

Principles of Education in reaction to attempts to make the function of schools to be career selection and training. These seven aims of education were (1) Health, (2) Command of fundamental processes, (3) Worthy home membership, (4) Vocation, (5) Citizenship, (6) Worthy use of leisure time, and (7) Ethical character.

Today most accredited schools have a published document which states the objectives of the school's educational program. Almost every one that I have seen is the same as the *Cardinal Principles* of 1918 but in more modern terminology. Usually a school must undergo a reevaluation every ten years to continue its accreditation. At this time committees are formed to revise and update the educational program. This begins with rewriting the objectives of the school. In almost all cases the objectives are rewritten to incorporate the latest educational jargon and the newest "buzz words" What does not seem to change is the actual objectives.

If you were to pull out your old high school handbook from your alma mater and read its educational objectives and compare them to those of the school in your community today, chances are that the objectives would be the same. Oh yes, there would be a change in the meaning of "fundamental processes" as we gain new knowledge and new tools, but the essence won't have changed.

Even the use of new tools is usually opposed by the schools. People do not want to change and often resist until they begin to look ridiculous. Let me just give you a few examples.

"Students today can't bark to calculate their problems. They depend upon their slates which are more expensive. What will they do when the slate is dropped and it breaks? They will be unable to write."
 – *Teachers Conference, 1703*

"Students today depend too much upon ink. They don't know how to use a pen knife to sharpen a pencil. Pen and ink will never replace the pencil."
 – *National Association of Teachers, 1907*

"Students today depend upon store brought ink. They don't know how to make their own. When they run out of ink, they will be unable to write words or ciphers until their next trip to the settlement. This is a sad commentary on modern times."

– *Rural American Teacher, 1929*

"Ball point pens will be the ruin of education in Our Country. Students use these devices and then throw them away! The American virtues of thrift and frugality are being discarded. Business will never allow this."

– *Federal Teacher, 1950*

"Calculators should not be allowed in the classroom. How will students ever learn the concepts of chemistry and physics if they are allowed to use calculators?"

– *Science Teachers Conference, 1975*

As you can determine from the above, changes are resisted by the education system until changing technology and society puts so much pressure on the system that it overwhelms the resistance. Many educational scholars have written that education reflects the society. There are others who believe that American education can be used to change or "improve" our society. In most cases, the most influential segment of society has already changed and is placing stress on the educational system (as well as other segments of society) to reflect this change.

Educational leaders are more than willing to step forward and take credit for an "improvement" in the current "crisis" in American society. Unfortunately, too many educational leaders believe their own press and begin to offer to solve the problems of American society. Schools cycle through programs that reflect the current crisis as popularized by the media. When we look at the history of schools, we see a cycle of programs that propose to solve the country's problems. Here are just a few of the more familiar:

Career education

Citizenship

Conflict resolution

Conservation education

Consumer education

Driver education

Drug education

Environmental education

Ethnic appreciation

Family education

Fine arts appreciation

Folk lore

Gun awareness

Health education

Sex education

Technology training

Work ethnic

"There ought to be a course" is the battle cry of every pressure group in this country. Not only should there be a course, but it should be *required* of every student in every school. One course is never enough. It soon turns into a program. As one of these types of programs go into a school, another fades out. These programs change names with each cycle. A program just about disappears when a pressure group appears, name is changed, and it is reintroduced as a "new" program that must be included in the school's curriculum. In large districts there are a core of "specialists" that seem to move from one of these program drives to another every couple of years.

On a larger scale, the entire American education system cycles through a series of objectives. The schools are America's way of solving whatever problems are thought to be critical in the era. The objectives of the education system cycle between citizenship objectives, vocational/job objectives, social agendas, and occasionally higher academic performance. The education system was used to "Americanize" the waves of immigrants in the early part of the last century. It became a vocational system during the depression days when marketable skills and work ethic was foremost. During the space race days, it was expected to produce more engineers and scientists. Shortly after that it was used to try to solve racial problems of the country.

—

When I was in school and when I first began teaching, students were segregated into "tracks" based on their academic performance. This was called "homogenous grouping" The best performing students were placed in the top track and the poorest performing students were assigned to the bottom track with one or two levels in-between.

For reasons discussed in the next chapter the reformers of education changed to "heterogeneous grouping" where students of all performance/ability levels are randomly assigned to classes. There no longer were high track/level and low level/track classes.

Suddenly there were new courses offered called "honors" courses and "star" for students who had demonstrated higher ability. These courses were followed by "advance placement (AP) "courses. This is just tracking under a different name.

But these were not enough for some people. Larger districts formed "magnet" schools. These schools were a special track school. So now there are "engineering "magnet schools, "performance" magnet schools, "academic" magnetic schools etc. These are special admit schools where students have to apply and are accepted based on their academic performance or, in some cases, they have to take an admissions test. In larger cities these schools take almost all of the top performing students out of the regular high schools.

The magnet schools did not do enough for the former middle track students. Parents were upset that they were in classes with students who didn't care about learning and could be disruptive. The charter school idea took hold. Charter schools were organized and funded in most major cities. Each charter school is a niche for a specific type of student. Most have rather small homogenous student bodies.

The educational system has resisted change again. Rather than a having different academic tracks within a school, the individual school choices available to students have become the academic/social/ethnic/economic tracks of the new century. Le Chatelier's principle prevails again.

—

Is it possible to significantly change the American education system? Everybody believes that education is important. I know of no politician who is "against" education. There are no organized groups that I know of who are against education. All seem to agree that it needs to be changed to improve the quality of education. This being the case, one would think that it would be easy to make significant and meaningful changes and improvements.

There is always a group of people who want to reform education. When you listen closely to the reformers, most of them usually want to return education to the way it was (as they remember it) when they were in school. These reform movements often have the most support and are successful in having an effect on the system. Just another example the Le Chatelier's principle operates in the educational system.

CHAPTER 7

Farber's Seventh Postulate

EDUCATIONAL THEORY FOLLOWS MONEY, NOT EDUCATIONAL RESEARCH

Everything has a cost. This is just as true in education as it is in other aspects of our world. When we follow the money, we learn how a business operates. Education is no different. School systems have only a certain amount of money to spend and must choose what to buy and what not to buy. Institutions, not unlike many people, often want to buy more than their budget will allow. Schools look for ways to lower their costs and ways to enhance their income to buy more things.

A corporation has to justify its expenditures to the directors and stockholders. It does this by showing how its purchases of materials, labor, equipment, etc. enhance its productivity and profitability. The balance sheet each quarter or year tells the stockholders how successfully the resources of the company have been used. When a company is not profitable, it will soon go out of business.

Schools do not have a profit and loss sheet. Schools don't even have a way of measuring their actual productivity. It typically takes twelve years for a child to earn a high school diploma. In this time period there are usually three changes of school superintendents and school boards. If this years' graduates lack in their preparation, the blame is usually placed on people who have long since moved on and the present school administration can claim that it has made improvements that will show up sometime in the future.

Schools do not have stockholders. In many cases they don't even know for sure who the stakeholders are in their particular educational institution. Elected school boards must face the voters but many school boards are appointed by other elected officials. I know of no state that requires even a small percentage of school board members to have children enrolled in the school system that they govern.[28] Private schools, colleges and universities have many different methods of forming their governing boards. Administrators appointed by boards have to justify their expenditures to these boards. Since there is usually no profit line in educational institutions, the administrators often use educational theory or "best practices" to explain how they are spending the money allotted to them to operate the school.

In the world of science, theories are developed to explain regularities which have withstood studies or experiments that have been repeated many times by different scientists. In the world of education, people look at where there is money to be gained or saved. Then they try to come up with a theory to justify making changes to chase the money. After they develop a workable theory, they search the archives of educational studies to find research to support the theory which they want to put into practice.

Textbook publishers, science equipment companies, electronics companies, etc. employ this tactic to sell to the schools. Schools want to extract more funds from the state or federal government and continuously alter their practices to maximize their income. School boards need new reasons to increase taxes.

The reality is that it is possible to find a "scientific study" to justify almost any practice or curriculum that exists in education. The administrators can decide what they want to do and, with a bit of research, find a

---

28 One wag suggested that the way to "fix" an urban school system would be to require all school board members have children in the school system and to enroll their children in the lowest performing schools of the system. I can't imagine the type of person who would even consider being on a school board with these conditions.

study that will show this to be a benefit to the students or school.

At this point it is necessary to take a closer look of how educational studies are done. Most educational studies are done by doctoral candidates. They are required to do an "original "scientific study in education and defend it before a committee. If they are successful in the defense of the study, they are awarded the doctoral degree.

These studies require two groups of students, a test group and a control group. The groups must be "identical." Since no two people are identical, even monozygotic twins, getting identical groups is difficult. The best way to cancel out individual differences is to have large groups. Medical studies use groups of a thousand or more to test a drug and still are often surprised by adverse side effects when the drug is approved and placed on the market. Then millions may take it and a hundred or so have a catastrophic side effect. A hundred out of a million is 0.0001. The point here is that applying the results of a study done using small groups of people to a much larger group will often produce many unexpected results.

Applying the methods of science to societal studies is fraught with pitfalls. The multi-ethnic and multicultural mix in school populations changes from year to year within a school and often changes from classroom to classroom. To take the results of a study done in one school, in one town or city and apply the results to another school in another location may or may not be appropriate.

A study can have internal and external validity. Internal validity means that if the study were done again under the same conditions, the results would be the same. Almost all studies done by universities have internal validity. External validity means that the same procedures can be applied in other situations and the results would be similar. Forecasting the external validity is, in my opinion, like forecasting the weather. The longer the range or wider the forecast, the less accurate the weather prediction will be.

The experimental group will be given the procedures, curriculum, etc. that is being tested, while the control group will receive whatever is presently the norm for this school. There is a common problem with all studies done with people, even drug studies-it is the placebo effect. When people think that they are getting something which will help them, they often improve. When students realize that they are getting a different treatment, they will often do better. Students often live up or down to teacher expectations. In one study, the researcher gave all the students a standard IQ test. He then randomly selected the names of some average students and told the teachers that the test showed that these students were very bright kids who would be "late bloomers." When he returned later, many of these students lived up to the random selection as "late bloomers." (Teachers do make a difference.)

The experimenter must determine how to measure any differences between the groups. It can be a test, an observation of skills, an interview etc. There are many varieties of pencil and paper tests, true false, multiple choice, short essays, interpreting drawings, or diagrams, etc. Students are often more successful on one form of test than another on the same subject. In all cases, students improve as they take the same type of test over and over again. When students take a series of tests written by the same person or group, they pick up on the ways questions are worded, which gives clues to the expected response.

We all have had the experience of hearing the results of polls taken by opposing political action groups. Each group does a poll and reports that the majority of respondents favor their position. Neither group is actually lying. The pollsters know they can obtain the desired results in their poll by the way they word their questions.

The publishers of textbooks and school curricular material fund many of the educational studies through grants to universities and individual professors and students. They are looking for educational research to help them promote their books and materials. They also advertise in educational journals. Studies that support their books will be published widely while others will languish on the dusty shelves of a university library.

What determines if one group performs significantly better than the other? The problem here is the definition of "significance." This is defined by the researcher. It could be at the 0.01 level which means one out of one hundred.

For a study to be considered acceptable in the world of science it has to be replicable, that is the study can be done again and again with the same results. You could possibly flip a coin one hundred times and get 80 heads and only 20 tails. If you repeat this coin flip, it is very unlikely that you will get the same results. When you do many, many 100-count coin flips, the average of the results will approach 50-50. Educational studies are seldom repeated for several reasons. Most are done by doctoral students who are required to do original research. This means that they must design a study that is unique rather than copy (plagiarize) the design of a study done by someone else. The "new" study will be reviewed by a committee of professors for the scientific validity of the design. This shows that the study has "internal validity." That means that all the variables are controlled so that, theoretically, if the study is repeated exactly under the same conditions with exactly the same types of students, the results *should be* the same. This does not speak to the external validity of the study. This means that if even one condition (variable) is different, the results *may be* different. Every experienced teacher knows that every class is different. The lesson which is great in one class can be a total dud in another. Once again, it is like flipping the coin a hundred times. Sometimes heads is strongly favored and other times tails will be favored.

There is a very basic problem in the fact that the vast majority of educational studies are required to be "original" by the fact that they are done by people hoping to earn a doctorate. Most never do another "valid" study in their career. The system of education research is actually stacked against the replication of studies. No educational journal is going to publish a replicated study that supports the results of a previous study. Professors must publish to keep their jobs and graduate students must do original studies. Science does not accept studies that are not replicated by others and education does not replicate most of its studies. You can see that there is a problem.

—

Now that I have bored you for a couple of pages in an attempt to explain how it is possible to find a scientifically valid educational study to support almost any practice or curriculum that a school wants to implement, it is time to move on to the realities of how educational institutions operate.

When I began my career as a science teacher the push was for more laboratory time for students. The students were to learn science by doing science. We were taught that the students could "discover" the laws and principles of science in the lab rather than having the teacher explain these in lecture. We were still in the post Sputnik era and the National Science Foundation, Defense Department and many other state and federal agencies were showering schools and science teachers with money for labs and lab equipment. The publishers and school science supply companies with government grants produced new science curricula with appropriate lab equipment to sell to the schools. We had ISCS, BSCS, ESCP, Chem Study, etc. The politicians wanted the schools to produce more scientists and engineers and were willing to pay the schools to do so.

When I accidentally discovered that the students in my school who took the traditional biology curriculum scored much higher than the BSCS students on the biology aptitude SAT test, I asked some questions. While I enjoyed the lab oriented approach to teaching science, I wanted to do what was best for the students. Could it be that we went too far in expecting students to "discover" the laws of science in labs. I was told by one of my graduate school professors that high school students would be able to "discover" Mendel's laws for themselves in a two hour lab. (It took Mendel over 6 years. I guess that he was a slow learner.)[29] I said that test results don't lie. I was told that tests are not a true measure of a students' science ability and knowledge. I realized that the studies that supported the new science curriculum

---

29 Mendel crossed 24,034 pea plants through several generations. He published two years after he completed his experiments.

were sometimes measuring something different than what the SAT exam measured. At the time I had no easy way of checking the original studies. The internet did not exist. This was before we even had pocket calculators.

—

Teachers are forever required to go to summer workshops and retraining in the in-service day sessions. Each year there seems to be some "new" method or approach that we are expected to learn and put into practice. Every one of these sessions seems to begin with someone telling us that this new method/approach has been "proven" by research. Following my fourth postulate, I ask to be given the original research so I can read it myself. Of course, they don't have it. Then I ask the workshop leader if they have a reference, title and author, so that I can look it up on the internet. The best the presenter can usually do is to say that they read an educational journal article that this "new" method was supported by research.

Reading the original research publication is not easy for most people. Just look up some doctoral dissertations and read them for fun. They are great remedies for insomnia. Most educational journalists just read the abstracts of the research. The educators that run the school systems only read the journals. The result is that no one really has the knowledge to determine the external validity of the research.

This pseudo-knowledge of research is nothing new. Most people know that the theory of evolution is based originally on Darwin's publication of "Origin of the Species." I found once that, in a room full of biology teachers, I was the only one who had actually read the book. They had only read what others have written about Darwin's theory.

—

One of the saddest sagas of how educational theory follows the money is that which has happened with special education over the years.

My state, like most states, recognized that special education needed to do more than placing students in regular classes. The department of education developed a set of regulations for special educational students. There were many studies that led to theories of how to better educate these students. The theory was that these students needed more individualized attention. They were intimidated by being in regular classes. They were embarrassed when they didn't understand things that the other students handled with seemly ease. They quit trying when they were continuously getting lower grades than their classmates. This led to low self-esteem and they would drop out of school whenever possible.

Chief among these regulations were that they were to be placed in smaller classes with specially trained teachers. The special ed class size in high school was limited to about 24 students. Normal classes were 33 students. All of this fit nicely with the educational theory of the time. Of course this is going to cost more. The state recognized this and agreed to give the schools an addition amount of money for each special educational student that they had in their school. That seemed to be a reasonable thing to do.

Schools hired teachers with special education certification and dedicated groups of classrooms to the special education program. The schools got the same amount of money for each special education student. Severely challenged students needed more that the mildly challenged student. The schools could not decrease the number of severely challenged, but found many ways to increase the number of mildly challenged. Educational studies kept finding more ways that students could be handicapped or challenged and the definition of special needs student continually expanded.

The schools had found a way to extract much more money from the state. I taught in a high school that has 2800 students on roll (attendance was something else). This school has almost 600 special educational students. That was about ¼ of the students who actually attended. State payments were based on actual attendance of the special educational student. Somehow our special students had better attendance than other students. When they were absent, personal calls were made to homes. Other students were given out of school suspensions for misbehavior. Different solutions were used with the special educational students.

Then the inevitable happened. The state budget appropriation for special education fell short of the commitment made to the schools. The schools were given IOUs as the department of Ed hoped for more money in the following year. Then it happened again the next year. The writing was on the wall. The school districts would need to come up with funds for the special education programs.

It was time for a new theory of how to educate special education students. Some people did a study where special education students were placed in regular classes and it was found that they learned more than those who remained in the special education classes. This was called "mainstreaming."

I'm sure that these studies were internally valid. With the expanded definition of "special education" there were many capable students who were labeled "special." There were other students who really needed the special attention. No one seemed to really read the studies or try to identify the students who could be successful when mainstreamed.

Within two years the special education department was reduced to almost nothing. The special ed teachers were either teaching regular classes or laid off. Teachers were told that the special students would be supported. There would be a "resource room" where teachers could go and meet with a former special education teacher to get help in meeting the needs of the mainstreamed students. The mainstreamed students could be scheduled for one period per day in the resource room if they needed help.

I was teaching an academic chemistry class of 33 students of which 4 or 5 were mainstreamed special students. Some special students were able to keep up. Two of them were reading on the second grade level. They could not read the captions on the illustrations in the textbook. They could not read lab procedure instructions. I was told that I should take 10 minutes day individually with these students. If I take 10 minutes every day out of a 46 minute class, the other 31 students lose the equivalent of one class period per week of instruction. Of course the academic teachers complained that their regular students were not going to be as well prepared for advanced studies.

Then things got more interesting. More studies were "discovered" that showed that mainstreamed special education students had lower self-esteem because they could be identified by their peers. This caused them to fall even further behind. We were told that we must do all that we can to prevent them from being identified.

The first thing was to cut the reading teachers for high school special ed students. When other students saw this on their classmates rosters or saw them go into the reading classrooms, it identified these students as special ed. Then the resource room and resource teachers seemed to disappear. I suppose that this saved the school even more money.

If all this was not enough, the next year the classroom teachers were not told which students were special education students. Only when a student was having difficulty and the teacher contacted a counselor or roster office, was the teacher told that the student had special needs.

Unfortunately the changes and counter changes in special education seemed to me to be more about following the money rather than the actual needs of the students. The parents of special needs children have become very politically active and a balance seems to have been restored that provides help to the children who actually need it.

—

A couple of decades ago most high schools had industrial arts programs, business programs and many had vocational education programs. These programs were designed to prepare students to enter the job market after graduation from high school. Public schools recognized that a sizable percentage of high school graduates would not be going on to further education immediately, if at all.

These programs could provide students with marketable skills by which they could gain entry level positions in local business and industry.

Business students learned typing, bookkeeping, office management and took courses in economics, finance and business law.

Industrial arts programs usually included print shop, wood shop, metal shop, electrical shop and auto shop. Home economics was also offered in most schools.

For students who wanted to actually learn a skill, the vocational education programs allowed students to spend a half day of each day or more in small group learning to be a pattern maker, mechanic, beautician , printer, electrician, carpenter, draftsman, machinist, chef, etc.

In the late twentieth century these programs became a financial problem for the schools. The vocational education programs were required to have a very low teacher student ratio. One instructor could not have more than 15 students at a time and this was enforced by the state and trade certification organizations. An academic teacher could have more than double the number of students in a class and required no expensive equipment to conduct class. A piece of chalk and a blackboard is sufficient.

Then the equipment used in the fields changed. Business educational programs required new expensive computers every few years. The old typewriters lasted a decade or more. The machine shop needed new computerized milling machines, etc. The auto shop needed computerized diagnostic equipment and emissions testing devises that had to be updated annually. Offset printing was not used anymore.

What were schools to do? These programs were costly to begin with and now they were getting even more costly. The solution, of course, is to have a new theory about what the student needs to be taught in high school. Research studies were found that concluded that the people who have earned college degrees earn more money than those who have only high school degrees. This is the solution. Prepare all the students for college. This is the least expensive way to operate the schools. All that is needed is one teacher, a piece of chalk and as many seats as you can cram into a classroom.

Schools closed all their business and industrial arts programs. There are a few vocational schools remaining, but these are usually a joint venture supported by several school districts.

Once again the education system is following the money rather than looking at the real needs of their students. One only has to look at the earnings of an electrician, carpenter, or plumber today to realize that it is possible to earn a good living without a college degree.

I was teaching in a school which had a good vocation education program. One of my better science students was also taking machine shop in the afternoons. I thought that I could get him into a good engineering program but he refused to even apply. He told me that he had an offer to start as an apprentice machinist which was more than the school was paying first year teachers. He then went on to calculate what he would make in the next four years and then added the cost of four years of college(without interest on student loans) to show me how far he would be ahead of his classmates who went to college. I couldn't argue with his logic.

Later I was teaching at an inner city school where all industrial arts and business programs had been shut down. In my chemistry class was a student who was already cutting hair and earning a barber's license. His goal was to have his own shop. He had to take chemistry, elementary functions, etc. but the school did not offer bookkeeping or business law anymore. He had to learn these things on his own. A few years later he had a successful shop—no thanks to his high school!

I taught in another inner city high school where all 2800 students on roll qualified for a free breakfast and lunch. These students came from families that often went without necessities and certainly did not have the means of paying for college tuition. Some of the top students did get scholarships to college and a few got athletic scholarships. The only way that these students could pay for college was to take out tens of thousands of dollars in student loans.

We all know of people who "worked" their way through college but this is not a reality for the B/C student from an inner city school. This student needs to have lots of study time to be successful in the rigorous courses required to earn a college degree. They do not have the time to both work at a job and have the study time they require.

Many students realize that the "everybody is going to college" program of high schools is not reality for them.[30] The dropout rate in these schools ought to be a clear indication that the college prep program is not of any interest or present use to these students.

There are some students who stay in school and graduate because they realize that a high school degree will be required for jobs beyond entry level. One such student was enrolled in my chemistry class. He was in an afternoon class, but did not attend very often. I kind of cornered him in the hallway one day and told him that there was no way he could learn enough to pass without attending the class. He politely explained that he had a job in the afternoon and left school at one o'clock every day. He understood that he would fail the two subjects that he had in the afternoon but that was okay. He would take those in summer school, which was always out by noon. He went on to explain that he was already making more than $2 over minimum wage as an assistant manager at a fast food chain. He would complete his high school only because managers were required to have a high school degree.

—

When I started teaching, most schools grouped students in classes by their ability and/or performance. This was called homogenous grouping. Students who wanted to learn and get ahead were grouped together and moved much more rapidly. Even the poor inner city schools had graduates who went on to be MDs, PhDs, astronauts, etc.

The other end of this spectrum was the bottom group. If a school had 10 classes in a grade, section 10 consisted of a group of students with almost

---

30 It is more difficult to fool students than adults. Adults can be "snowed" by big words and complex sentences. Students ignore the verbiage and watch what is actually happening.

no interest in learning. Teachers did not want to be assigned to teach the bottom sections. Usually the newest teacher was assigned the bottom sections. My first teaching roster consisted of five classes on three grade levels and three bottom sections.

What I am describing here is the extreme. Most schools grouped students into three or four "tracks" Only the top track was considered "college bound." The next track could go to college but not top schools. The other tracks were considered prepared for technical schools or entering the work force directly from high school.

Two major forces worked to change this system.

One was the theory that all students should be prepared for college. Why have different tracks when everyone was going to get the same preparation. The schools were having young teachers quit because the bottom track/sections consisted of students who were more difficult to control, let alone teach the prescribed curriculum. The dilution of problem students into classes of more motivated students was thought to be the solution of handling these more troubling students.

The second force was racial balancing. The politicians and lawyers who actually control the schools became aware that each individual track did not reflect the racial mix of the school.

Heterogeneous grouping of students suddenly became the rule. It was an inexpensive solution to students who were harder to control. The schools didn't have to spend money to motivate more minority students to earn seats in the top track. Is it better for the students? That was not the question. If there are problems, it is up to us teachers to find the solutions

—

When students were homogeneously grouped, the theory was that students with nearly equal ability could compete with each other. The competition would bring out the best in the homogenous class. All students would work because the homogenous grouping made a more level playing field within the classroom. The theory was that everyone would learn more. We did not have to worry that always being so far behind the others that he/she would develop low self-esteem and give up.

Heterogeneous grouping changed that almost level playing field. Competition will always be won by the same students and other students will always be left in the dust.

Time for a new theory. "Research has shown that students learn more when working in groups." Suddenly teachers are told that students must work in groups to learn. The buzz term becomes "cooperative learning."

Teachers are instructed on how to place students in groups. Each group must have one A and one D/F student and an equal number of B and C students. The group will work on assignments together and everyone in the group will receive the same grade.

The theory is that the students who want good grades will teach the subject to other students. In a teacher workshop we were told that students can explain the subject to other students better than teachers can explain it. (After all those years I spent studying science, now I am told that a student can explain it better. Maybe the school does not need to hire teachers at all.) This "new" method would allow us to successfully teach students functioning at vastly different levels in the same classroom at the same time.[31]

—

Math is a real problem for textbook publishers. The problem is that the subject does not change. There is an absolute right answer for each arithmetic problem that does not change from decade or even century to century. The same textbook can be used for decades to teach basic arithmetic

---

31 This model is not new. It was based on the one room school of the 1800s. The teacher taught the more advanced students who taught the younger students who taught the youngest students. There is little new in education, it just recycles under a new name.

and algebra. Experienced math teachers usually find a textbook with clear explanations, good examples, and plenty of practice problems that works for their students. Once they find such a text, they want to keep using this textbook as long as possible. I have seen books almost 20 years old being used in a math classroom. This creates a problem for textbook publishers.

Publishers would like schools to buy all new books every 4-5 years. They actually charge more for older books than the newest books. They want to discourage schools from buying "fill in" books to replace only the books that have been lost or damaged. Selling new math books is more challenging than selling science books. Everyone knows that science is constantly changing. Many new discoveries are made every year. A science book is 2–4 years out of date on the day that it is published so it is easy to convince schools to continuously buy new science books. The multiplication tables don't change. Why would a school need to buy all new arithmetic books?

The solution to the problem of selling new math books was simple. Develop a new theory of how to teach math and sell new books that use the new educational theory. The publishers went to work and developed many new theories and curriculums to sell their wares. There seems to be a "new" math every few years. Parents get confused trying to help their children with their basic math homework. Teachers have to be re-educated.[32] When a publisher gets a state department of education to adopt its "new" math curriculum, it is like winning a lottery.

—

The scheduling of classes in a middle or high school has always been a challenge. Almost everyone is unhappy with their schedule of classes—students and teachers alike. Schedules are driven by many factors.

The student is required to be enrolled is a specific number of required

---

32   This works to support state colleges of education. Teachers are required to pay for more graduate courses to learn how to teach the new math curriculum.

courses each year. The number and type of course required is subject to change by the state or local school board at any time. There is always someone or group lobbying for another "required" course. The politicians tell us that the solution to every problem of society is to add another course in the schools. If there is money available to throw at a problem, you can bet that schools will put their hands out to catch that money.

Teacher contracts limit the number of consecutive classes that they are required to teach. It also requires that they be given a lunch break and some time to prepare lessons, grade papers, contact parents, meet with counselors, parents, other teachers, etc.

Some courses require two consecutive periods or more. Science lab experiments usually require more than an hour to complete. Industrial arts require longer blocks of time. Often physical education requires additional time for students to change clothes and clean up.

There have been many studies of the attention span of students of all ages. I have not found a single one that concluded that the attention span of students is 45 minutes or more. Such educational studies are not really considered in building school schedules.

Developing a schedule for a school is always a compromise between many factors. Naturally, cost is the major factor. The efficient use of time and facilities is important. The larger buildings may require more time between classes because students as well as faculty may have long distances between classrooms. A longer time between classes means that there will be more student interaction in the hallways which can lead to another set of problems.

The typical high school student college prep course requirements are English, math, social studies, science, foreign language and physical education. This requires 6 class periods. The students are encouraged to take an elective course each year. This means that the school day must allow for 7 or more class periods.

Then someone came up with a new idea. Why not have only 4 class periods in a school day? This was called the "block" schedule. The student would take a subject for ½ of the school year but would have the same in class time as the traditional schedule provides in a year. This schedule was more efficient since there were fewer class changes and time spent in the hallways. Of course this cut down on the problems that occur in the halls during the changing of classes.

The theory was that the students would learn more because they would not be studying so many different subjects at the same time. We were told that research studies showed that the students did better and there were few student discipline problems. We could see some real advantages for some of our students. I could envision students doing much better in foreign language. I thought that we would decrease the failure rate in math courses. There would be less lab time in science and some science classes would not have access to labs.[33]

However, upon doing our own review of research and contacting teachers in schools using this schedule, we discovered that students did not do as well in standardized tests and SAT tests.

Then we found the real reason that the school district wanted to convert all the schools to this schedule. In my school district the teachers' contract permitted high school teachers to be assigned 5 teaching periods per day. This means that the teacher will teach five courses per year. With the block schedule, teachers would teach 3 periods per day. This means that they would in effect teach 6 courses per year. Suddenly the reason for the block schedule became clear.

The block schedule was short lived. The movement for state wide standardized testing killed it. The students on the block schedule did not score as well on standardized tests. The schools were required to bring up the student test scores.

---

33 I wrote a chemistry lab manual specifically for block scheduled chemistry classes that did not have access to chemicals and labs. It used things that could be found in hardware stores and supermarkets. This manual, "Off the Shelf Chemistry Lab," is still used by some home schoolers.

—

Large city school systems may have an enrollment of over 100 thousand students. Their cost per student usually exceeds $10,000. City systems serve students with many problems. Some may not understand English. There are students who often are absent because of poor living conditions. It does not seem unreasonable to have one student out of twenty fail for the year in a city system. It costs an additional $10,000 each time a student repeats a grade. In a hundred thousand student school system a failure rate of one out of twenty students' amounts to five thousand students. This effectively increases the enrollment of the system by this number. When a system spends $10,000 per year per student, this increases the annual cost by fifty million dollars.

The potential money that student failures can cost a school system means that the educational system needs to find a theory that will allow all students to pass each year. Classroom teachers will argue that the student does not "know" enough to move to the next grade. This student is behind the other students in reading or math skills. This student will be lost and become frustrated. He or she may act out disruptively. All seem to be valid reasons to have a student repeat a grade.

However, when this amount of money is at risk, you must forget about what is best for the education of the student. There will be a theory found to protect the school systems from this financial dilemma.

Over the years there have been many, many theories touted by educators to justify moving students on to the next grade without regard for their skills or knowledge. All sorts of "social promotion" theories have been used. A book "Schools Without Failure" was very popular. Teachers were told to use "alternate assessments" Student drawings rather than knowledge or skill measuring tests were used to promote students.

Tenured teachers are a tough group to control. They are dedicated to helping students and do not want to place them in harm's way. They try to protect students from having unrealistic demands placed on them.

Teachers will see that a student will be expected to do work at a level on which he/she can not function and they will do their best to protect the student by giving that student more time to reach that level. This often means having the student repeat the grade level.

School administrators try to put pressure on teachers and principals to make sure that all students pass at the end of the year. Principals, by law, have the power to change the grades given by teachers. They do it more often than most of the public realize. Unionized teachers sometimes publicly complain. They seldom get much support.[34]

The city system where I taught had a rule at one time that a student could be held back only once in the first eight years. This required the principals to override the teacher's grades and recommendations for many struggling students.

An alternate solution was to label a student "special." This created the large number of special education students, which was discussed earlier.

"No child left behind" with its standardized testing and reporting is a direct attack on the economics of the present systems of promotion and graduation found in many schools. It appears to be universally opposed by school boards, administrators and teacher groups. As the bills for its implementation come due there will be many new theories presented to try to get around it.

—

Whenever there is an economic downturn and the schools *really* don't have the money to make ends meet, they dust off an old idea. It is the theory that the people actually doing a job know more about how to do the job than their bosses. This theory tells us that if the people doing the job are given the freedom to make choices about how to do the job and what is needed to accomplish

34   See the tenth postulate: "Education is the only business where the customer is satisfied with less and less product."

their tasks, they will find ways to do the job better and more efficiently. In education this is usually called something like "teacher empowerment."

Teacher empowerment usually shows up when a school needs to cut the classroom supply budget or reduce the number of teachers. No one wants to make these decisions. The schools are political and no politician ever got re-elected by cutting jobs or benefits.[35] This is a no win situation. A great answer to this situation is to pass the decision to someone else. In government the elected official passes the problem on when he/she retires or is elected to another office. The answer in schools is to pass the problem onto the teachers (or teacher unions) through some sort of teacher empowerment.

Teacher empowerment theories will evaporate as quickly as a school finds extra money to spend.

Teachers also need to be aware of the word "*professional*." The dictionary may define it as "engaged in one of the learned professions for gain or livelihood" or "engaged in by persons receiving financial return."

In education, the term" professional" usually means that the teachers are being asked/told to do additional jobs for free. It, like teacher empowerment, is dangled in front of teachers whenever there is a lack of funds.

—

Our world is based on economics. This is the root of most wars. Most of our major life decisions have an economic component. It would be very naïve to think that education is any different. When I say that education follows the money, it is not a criticism of the educational system. It is a reality that teachers must recognize and learn how to live with it. It follows the purpose of this book, which is to provide young teachers with information that they did not receive in the college of education.

---

35 People can get elected by promising to reduce government employees and government spending but if they actually do so, they will not get re-elected. Schools, like government, tend to continually grow until disaster strikes.

CHAPTER 8

Farber's Eighth Postulate

THE PRIMARY FUNCTION OF MOST SCHOOLS IS DAYCARE, NOT EDUCATION

This is a chapter that I loathe to write. I include it only because I wish to be honest with the people who may be reading this book in preparation to become teachers. It is one chapter which does not contain any humor. If you are reading this book for entertainment, I suggest that you skip this chapter. Most teachers find this very difficult to accept after all the indoctrination needed to earn a teaching certificate. Physical education teachers understand and accept this postulate. Which may explain why so many of them are successful in moving into administrative jobs such as building principal and district superintendent.

Schools have always been more than a place where kids learn the three R's. Schools have Americanized the waves of immigrants. They have been the true melting pots in larger cities. Schools are the instruments of social change and have been the front line in the fight against racial and ethical prejudice. These are all important and worthwhile functions of our educational institutions.

I didn't realize the importance of schools as daycare centers until I was waiting in a checkout line one day when school had been cancelled because of snow. I found myself listening to several women discussing all the inconveniences they had suffered that morning because schools had been closed. They were talking about how conditions were not *really* that bad etc. This seemed incredible to me. I was thinking that these people don't seem to care about their children.

The previous year in my district, on a day with less snow than we had today, a city bus skidded over a curb and killed a child waiting for a school bus. School officials were blasted in the media for putting children at risk by not closing schools.

Pity the superintendents. They are in a no win situation. If children are injured or worse, the school district is liable. If parents must stay home from jobs to care for their children, they are angry at the superintendent. One superintendent thought that he could avoid some of the parental wrath by announcing school closings the evening before, based on the weather prediction. This gave parents time to make arrangements for the supervision of their children. As you have by now realized, this only worked until the weather prediction was wrong.[36]

The most telling situation is in a school district where 95% of the students are bussed to school. On days when the snow makes traveling dangerous, schools remain *"open with no transportation."*

What does this tell you about the function of the school? It means that the highly trained and educated staff will function as baby-sitters for any student who is dropped off at the schoolhouse. Children will be dropped off and picked up anytime throughout the normal school hours. The majority of children will not be present and late arrivals and early pickups will constantly disrupt activities. Naturally, the school officials will claim that there is a "meaningful educational" program taking place. If you truly believe this, call me, I can make you a great deal on a bridge in Brooklyn.

If you are too old to remember what school was like when it was open in spite of heavy snow, let me refresh your memory. If you arrived more or

---

36 Assign the students to graph 5 or 10 day weather forecasts versus actual weather for a month. It is a very interesting experience for the students. However you can forget about students taking the predictions of global warming seriously later in the school year. Further, when the students realize that, as a weatherman, you can be wrong again and again and still not be fired, they may decide to major in meteorology.

less on time, you were directed to the gym or auditorium. You remained there for most of the morning or until all of the school buses and most of the teachers arrived. In class, teachers did not cover any new material because too many students were missing. They just reviewed or gave you boring drill work. A few presented "enrichment" material that may have been interesting but would not show up on any tests. There were no substitutes for teachers who were absent and there were a higher than average number of teachers out "sick." Some teachers "covered" two classes at a time if there was enough space for everyone in one room. Classes of other absent teachers were sent to areas, which functioned as holding tanks, such as the cafeteria or auditorium. The students were bored and creating their own fun. The students gave any teacher trying to run a normal class a difficult time. Many teachers, in order to avoid discipline problems, gave in to students who did not want to do any educational work that day.

—

The true history of American education tells us that it has almost never been about education. The earliest education in the colonies was aimed at social concerns. The "foundation of the American public school system" was a 1647 law enacted by the Massachusetts Bay Colony. It was known as the "Old Deluder Satan Law." This law reads:

"It being one chief project of that old deluder Satan to keep men from the knowledge of the scriptures, as in former times by keeping them in an unknown tongue, so in these later times by persuading from the use of tongues, (that so at least the true sense and meaning of the original might be clouded by false glosses of saint-seeming deceivers,)-(to the end) that learning may not be buried in the grave of our fathers in church and commonwealth, the Lord assisting our endeavor.

"It is therefore ordered, that every township in this Jurisdiction, after the Lord had increased them to the number of 50 householders, shall forthwith appoint one within their town to teach all such children as shall resort

to him, to write and read ..."

In other words, the function of education was to teach the children to read the Bible.[37]

Beginning in the late 1960s more women began to work outside of the home. Before this time educated women were directed toward careers in health care or education. Opportunities in other fields were limited. There were positive changes in the economic opportunities for women. The domino effect of these opportunities gradually changed from opportunities to necessities. The cost of houses increased to reflect the buying power of a two-income family. Public transit did not keep pace with suburban sprawl and often two cars were needed to commute to two widely separated places of work. The number of single parent families skyrocketed. When children reached school age, mother went back to being a wage earner if she did not already have a job outside of the home. In most cases, there was no adult at home to care for children. When they were sick or school was closed, someone had to be absent from their job, schedules had to be rearranged, or arrangements made with friends or relatives.

We are told that times have changed. Many groups are now advocating year round schools. They argue that we are no longer an agricultural society where children are needed to help on the farm in the summer. This has been true for almost a century. Why do we suddenly need to make a change? Others will argue that our children need more time in school to compete in the world economy. They point to Asian and European education systems and tell us that they are doing a better job.

All of this is just a smoke screen. Well, times have changed indeed. But let's be honest, those advocating year round schools want more public funded daycare, not better education.

Today most young couples depend on having two salaries. When they have children, they face the prospect of losing one of the salaries. The cost

---

37 How times have changed! Today a teacher, in some public schools, could be fired for Bible reading in class.

of placing a child in daycare is a major expense. When the second child comes along, the daycare cost may approach the take-home pay of one of the parents. When the children reach school age, it is a major financial relief for many families. They are free of the expense of daycare. School is, in effect, free daycare.

There are programs like "head start" to provide preschool daycare for many families that can't afford it. These programs are billed as educational boosters for children. While studies show that the children have an educational benefit when they begin school, long term studies indicate that the do not retain the benefit in the higher grades.[38]

The one problem that remains is that the school day is not as long as most people's working day. Some couples solve this by working different schedules. Those who can't adjust their schedules and single parent families have a real problem. Many schools and organizations are now providing "after school" care. These programs come at a cost to the parents. These parents would like to have a school day that actually extends beyond the working day. They need commuting time as well as working time coverage for their children. They will embrace any excuse to lengthen the school's hours.

Summer vacation is another financial burden on middle class families with young children. They need to have a safe supervised environment for their children. In the last decade there has been a proliferation of summer day camps. These are often under the guise of educational camps. Other camps are just recreational programs. The cost of these camps put an additional dent in the family budget.

Many school districts offer summer school programs for students who have failed subjects or need remedial help. Some schools offer "enrichment" educational programs. I have had students plead with me to give them a failing grade so that they can attend a free summer school program. They rather be in a safe school environment than whatever their families

---

38 The home environment remains the best predictor of a child's success in school.

could provide for the summer This urban school district only could afford, or could get state funding for, programs that would allow students to make up failed subjects. The district and state were well aware of the cost of a student spending an extra year or two in school. It made economic sense[39] to provide summer school for children who needed remedial help and/or needed to make up course failures.

—

Let's take a closer look at the "better" education systems in other parts of the world. In the British system, there is a large percentage of students who drop out of school. This is far more than our worst schools. But in England they don't call them dropouts. When students reach the age of 14 they are given a test to determine whether they will be continued in school or join the work force. Those who do not qualify for more schooling, are given skills training as required to enter the job market. The same type of thinning out of the less qualified is standard procedure in most of Europe. The American education system has as its goal to have 100% of the children achieve at least a high school degree. Of course, our high school students have a test average below the upper level of the European students who attend high school. If you took the average IQ of American high school students, it would be below the average IQ of the European high school student. Does that mean that Americans are dumber? No, it just means that our high schools are more inclusive.

At every level, students in other countries have more pressure. They know that if they don't pass certain tests, they will be denied entrance into high school and beyond. In Japan, in particular, this results in a high suicide rate of students. Is this what we want? Do parents want to spend evenings and weekends helping their children study and doing rigorous

---

39   See Farber's seventh postulate.

homework assignments?

Do the Japanese build schools with large gymnasiums, pools, and playing fields? Do their children spend time playing games and sports. Look closely at our schools. Calculate the percent of the school budget that goes to construct and maintain the gyms and fields. Then add in the salaries of the staff needed for the physical education and sports programs. This is a major chunk of the school budget. But think of the alternative. Imagine that the school board built schools with no gyms or playing fields. They did not hire any physical education teachers or coaches. All the students and staff would be required to line up in the classrooms or hallways and do calisthenics for twenty minutes twice a day. The students would get as much or more exercise than students in other schools. The school district would have money to significantly reduce class size and provide more technology. The students would most likely learn more and score higher on all standardized tests. But the students would not be happy and the community would be up in arms. No school board in America could get away with such a thing. This is because education is not the primary function of American schools.

In many urban settings, the school building has the duel function as a daycare for children by day and a community center in the evenings and weekends. The school administrators and politicians encourage the use of the buildings, playing fields and gyms by the adult community. This is a way of getting community support for a school that is not necessarily doing a very good job preparing students for life in the real world.

Once upon a time, schools were devoted to teaching the three R's: reading, 'riting, and 'rithmetic.[40] Today our schools revolve around the three S's: sound, socializing, and sports. In the upper grades it is streamlined to

---

40 I use *"Once upon a time"* deliberately because I have no way of knowing if it was ever true. It is part of our American folklore. The only people who seem to remember it are the same folks who also remember walking five miles through snow, up hill both ways, to attend school.

sound, sex, and sports.

Students are excused from academic classes to play sports. Even when a team has a "home" event, the team members are excused from classes to get prepared for their game or meet. Teachers who are also coaches are excused from teaching their late afternoon classes so that they can prepare for their sports event. Other teachers are assigned to "cover" the coach's afternoon classes. This is usually without any additional compensation but the coaching teacher receives extra compensation for having coaching duties. Most of the time the "covered" classes will be assigned "busy" work. The class will not have a lesson that will advance the students academically.

Cheerleaders and band members are also often excused from classes to support the sports teams. Lots of sound is needed to support the teams.

I've been in teacher workshops where it was suggested that we play music as the students enter our classrooms. This is supposed to make them cheerful and more receptive to learning. The music stops when the lesson begins. This would be the signal for them to get in their seats and settle down. Some educators think that we should play music during exams to allow the students to relax and do better on the exam. Of course, agreeing on the music could be a major problem. I suggested that we play classical music in the school hallways which may drive some of our hall wandering students into classrooms.

Once again I suggest that when one wants to know the true purpose of an organization, one should follow the dollar. As mentioned above, a very large part of our school funds are spent on sports related facilities, salaries, and equipment. If the school district is a bit short, the parents will organize fund raisers for new band uniforms, football equipment, bleachers, etc. When was there ever a fund raiser for new microscopes, dictionaries, or history books?

In one school we returned from summer vacation to find that there was a leak in the gym roof. Rain water had flooded a section of the gym floor and it had warped. When this happened in a classroom, the damaged area was cordoned off and we had to just work around it, sometimes for years. Not so in the gym. The school district came up with hundreds of thousands of dollars to repair the gym roof and replace the entire floor. This was done immediately. The entire floor was removed and replaced in what seemed record time for any school maintenance or repair project. Meanwhile we hadn't seen any significant money available for several years to buy new books or science equipment. In this large high school sports were far more important than academics when one followed the money.

Several years later I was teaching at an academic magnet school. One Monday morning we arrived to school to find that a water pipe burst in the gym. The floor was covered with six inches of water. Once again the district had no trouble finding the money to replace the gym floor, but never had the money to repair the plumbing in the old chemistry labs or renovate the library. If we wanted those things done, we would have to raise the money from alumni and parents.

Having worked in education for many decades, I have learned to read between the lines when a school board does not have sufficient income to balance the budget. When the school board wants to raise taxes, it announces that it will balance the budget by cutting *extracurricular* activities such as band, football, or other high profile extracurricular activities. If you really think about the meaning of the word "extracurricular," these activities are not part of the things needed for the educational program. Almost without fail, the parents get upset and begin lobbying for a tax increase. On one occasion, I remember a politician decrying that without the sports program, minority children could not go to college. I thought that this was an extremely insulting remark and expected a backlash from minority organizations. Wrong! These organizations rallied behind the tax increase.

When the school board is not in the mood to raise taxes the target of budget cuts is different. The first thing is that they cut library book purchases, library hours, and librarians. They will postpone buying new textbooks and have old books rebound. Then they cut counselors, reading specialists, art teachers, music instructors and orchestra. Very few people seem to care about the school library. The only time that it is important is when the school's decade long accreditation is up for renewal. The parents are told that every teacher is a counselor and a reading teacher. Instrumental music lessons affect only a few students, and the orchestra does not play at sports events. The marching band is an adjunct to the sports program so, it is protected. The cuts take effect and school opens as if nothing important is missing. These cuts do not affect the three S's. The school will not have any difficulty meeting its primary function: daycare.

—

A function of all schools today is seeing that the students are fed. Most urban schools have breakfast and lunch programs. They will serve dinner as soon as the school hours are increased an hour or two. If a certain percentage of the students qualify for the free breakfast/lunch program, the entire school population gets free food. The federal programs reward the schools that pass out the most student meals. In many schools people are paid to hand out packaged breakfast food and juice as the children enter the building. The result is that in some schools the students can not refuse the food.[41] There are no major federal programs that provide the urban students with textbooks, notebooks, calculators or other educational materials. Feeding students, a daycare function, comes first; educational materials may occasionally come to these schools via federal programs.

—

In most urban school districts, *social promotion* is practiced. In some districts it is done quietly while others have a clearly stated policy. In the urban district where I taught, the policy was that no student may be held back more than once in the first eight grades. This means that students

---

41 Students are told that they don't have to eat the food, just take it. The result is often a mess in hallways and classrooms.

are promoted each year regardless of their reading, writing or math skills (the three R's of the old school). In fact, they can not be held back for lack of attendance.

Is this an educational program? The public stance of the school district is "Yes." There are all kinds of convoluted reasons to justify the policy. None of the justifications look at the effect on the majority of students, the teachers, or the educational tone of the school. This is not important. The social aspects of promotion have much more weight than educational difficulties that are created when unqualified students are pushed through the system.

Let's look at the other side of this coin. If there are students who are a grade level or two behind their peers in their academic skills, it stands to reason that there are some students every year who are a grade or two *ahead* of their peers. Logically[42] they should be allowed to skip a grade. This would make good sense educationally. This would allow these students to learn more rather than being bored and held back by sitting in classes where the teacher is presenting things that they already know and understand. So tell me, how many students skipped a grade in your local public school last year? My guess is none. If there is an exception, I'll bet that it was because of the insistence of a pushy parent rather than something the school system did as a matter of policy. If education were the primary function of the school, students who are significantly behind their peers would not be promoted and students who are significantly ahead of their peers would skip grades. Bright students are prevented from advancing more rapidly for the same social reasons as given for promoting unqualified students. Education is secondary.

In high school students must sit through the required courses even if they already know the subject. There is no method to allow advanced and bright students to "test out" of a course and receive credit toward graduation. In schools today we have many students who are immigrants and are

---

42   A violation of Farber's first postulate.

fluent in languages other than English. These students are "required" to take two years of a second language to meet the graduation requirements of "academic" high schools. Some of these students know the foreign language better than the teacher. The schools will not allow them to just take a pass/fail test in their native language and give them credit toward graduation. The schools won't even exempt them from taking a foreign language course. These students could benefit from taking extra elective courses of their choosing, but that will not be allowed. Once again, logic has no place in education.

Math appears to be the only exception. This is because there is a concise correct answer to each problem. In other disciplines we can't agree on what questions to ask the students let alone what is an acceptable response. Students can advance more rapidity through high school and college math by testing out of lower level courses.

Do you remember how many times you studied the same era of history through your twelve years of public education? There must be many students who could test out of "American history" by the time that they reach high school, but they will never be given that opportunity. The same could be said for "general science" as well as basic "English" courses. No, schools are designed to keep kids occupied within the confines of a designated building.

One of the dirty little secrets of our schools is that kids *are permitted to drop out of education.* The emphasis in education is to "stay in school." This does not mean that they must continue to get an education. Urban schools are under so much pressure so much to keep kids in school that they continue keeping kids enrolled as long as they show up occasionally. There are students who attend only a few days a month. The days that they do attend, they may spend most of their time in the lunch room or wandering the halls.

One trick that urban schools use is to take the official attendance the period just before the first lunch period. You may remember homeroom (now advisory period) as the room that you were assigned to be in every morning while waiting for other students and busses to arrive. In schools with attendance problems, students go directly to their classes and this homeroom period may be in mid-morning.

One year I had a girl in my ninth grade advisory that was in the ninth grade for the *fifth* year. She seldom attended more than one day per week. She did not have any known health problems that could account for her absences. Sometimes I did not see her for more than two weeks. She was older than many of our 12th grade students, but the school refused to expel her or take her off the roll.

There are students who attend regularly but seldom go to class. When teachers complain too loudly, they are usually told that it is their fault.[43] It is their job to motivate students and to make the class interesting so that students want to attend. In many schools there are rules that prohibit a teacher from making behavior (bad) a part of a student's grade. Lack of attendance is then interpreted as "bad behavior" thus it can not be used to "fail" a student. On the other hand, if a teacher wants to pass a student who is not doing well, good attendance can be interpreted as "effort" and used as part of the grade.

In our many "in service days" we were encouraged to use methods by which all students would receive a passing grade even if they didn't do much work. We were told that students should always work in groups and that everyone in the group should receive the same grade. Of course this system would not work as the administrators wanted if students were allowed to choose their groups. The students knew who would do the work and who would not. The nonworking students would be excluded by their

---

43 There is a simple logical solution to high school students who cut classes. These students can be assigned to a classroom and would never change rooms. The subject teachers would rotate to the classroom. The only way they could get reinstated in regular classes would be demonstrating maturity and responsibility. This would be measured by earning passing grades, good attendance and being on time for school. Instituting such a program would violate Farber's first postulate.

peers who actually wanted to earn better grades. The teachers were given instructions to place at least on A student in each group and spread out the low performing students into different groups. This system allows students who simply attend school to get passing grades.

The message is clear, attendance is important, learning is secondary.

I was teaching in one school where the school instituted "daycare" for student's babies so that they continued their education. It seemed like a reasonable idea to the teachers but the number of students with babies far exceeded the capacity of the day care center. The teachers proposed that we form a committee to determine which students would be qualified to put their children in this free day care program. The teachers naively thought that students should earn this privilege by attendance and grades. We were abruptly told that this was none of our business. We were not allowed any input into the operation of this program. Now we had students who were not attending class with the excuse that they were visiting their children in day care. Then we became aware that students, who were marked absent for the day, had children in the daycare. This soon became a problem for the daycare workers. At the end of the school day mothers often did not pick up their children. Students had dropped off their children and gone out for the day, visiting friends, shopping, etc. and missed the public bus back to the school.

—

At one time we considered 18 year olds to be adults. When they went to college they were referred to as college men and women. They were expected to finish college in four years. This is no longer true. We have used college to extend childhood several years. We now call college students "college kids." Many of them spend five or six years to earn what we use to consider a four year degree. Childhood has been extended almost to the mid-twenties. College functions as a daycare service for these older children. It does not seem to matter what they take in college or how many times they change their major. They enroll in courses and sit in classrooms with little or no idea of what they want to do for a living. This keeps many colleges, especially community colleges, filled with students. Many of these students are not ready or willing or able to get a paying job. Their families keep paying the college bills for lucky ones or they pile up large student loans. The attendance and promotion policies of many high schools do not instill responsible attitudes into their students. School districts have curtailed or eliminated business and technical programs. Most companies do not accept recent high school graduates into training programs that prepare them for better paying jobs. The combination or lack of skills and "work ethnic" limits too many high school graduates to minimum wage jobs. For these students and their families, college is just a very expensive daycare service until they develop the skills and attitudes needed to earn a living wage.

CHAPTER 9

Farber's Ninth Postulate

EDUCATION IS RUN BY POLITICIANS AND LAWYERS, NOT EDUCATORS

One of the things that many teachers do not realize is that education is not run by educators. They have spent countless hours in both undergraduate and graduate education course where they are taught methods of planning and executing an educational curriculum. They have read and discussed many books about the philosophy of education going back to Plato and the Greek philosophers. They have seen many different organizational diagrams of the various people or groups involved in planning a school curriculum. They have been taught that educators are empowered to plan, develop and deliver an educational system. They are so wrong.

Public schools, community colleges and state universities are under the direct control of politicians. The state departments of education are controlled by politicians. The departments of education license all the private schools, charter schools and private colleges. Both the state and federal government control schools through grants and certification of their programs.

Teacher unions realized this immediately. If they wanted concessions for their members, they had to work with the politicians. Teacher unions quickly became the most politically active of all the unions. We hear teacher unions and teachers attacked regularly by politicians who have had a falling out with the teacher unions. Other unions have to negotiate with business people and stockholders of corporations. They do not have to be directly involved with politics. We don't hear about as many attacks on them by our elected officials.

There are no educational requirements to be elected or appointed to a school board in most states. There is always an exception somewhere but I don't know of one. People will get upset with the school because their kid got a poor grade or didn't make the football team. They run for school board, get elected and start making school policy. Jimmy Carter started his political career on a school board.

Public officials are always concerned about their image. They do things and make decisions often based on how they think it will affect their public image.

At one time in my city the newspapers ran some articles critical of the academic rigor of the high schools. The school board responded by requiring all students to pass four years of math and science in order to graduate high school. At the time most students took only two years of science and two of math. The politicians running the schools never asked if this requirement was realistic. They never inquired if the school district had enough certified math and science teachers to teach the addition sections (it didn't). They did not ask if the students were interested in taking these courses. They didn't ask if the students had the preparation to be successful in these courses.

The politicians got what they wanted. They were publicly lauded for strengthening the academics of the public schools. The school administrators scrambled to hire more math and science teachers. They had to make massive purchases of new textbooks and science supplies. They had to drop other courses out of the school curriculum to make time for the additional science and math courses. This also meant that other teachers were laid off if another position could not be found (or created) for them. A year or two later the school district watched the graduation rate plummet and the dropout rate climb. Schools quietly instituted "alternate" science and math courses.

—

What is allowed to be taught or discussed in classes is determined by politicians. It can be changed 180 degrees in a year or two. Some subject areas have much closer scrutiny than others. Politicians usually don't care what we teach in math, chemistry, or physics but biology may be another story. Social studies and health are often watched more closely.

In a school where I taught, one of the health teachers deviated from the proscribed curriculum. She was concerned because members of our high school had over 100 live births per year. Along with this high pregnancy rate came the threat of a high rate of sexually transmitted disease. The teacher developed and taught a unit on birth control and safe sex. Word leaked out about this. The teacher received a letter, which was placed in her employee file, ordering her to stop teaching this immediately. It went on to say that if she was ever found teaching or discussing this topic again, that she would be summarily fired.

Two years later the AIDS scare hit the headlines. The politicians who ran the school system wanted to look like leaders in the fight against this deadly epidemic. This same health teacher now received a memo *requiring* her to teach a unit on safe sex and birth control to all of her health students.

A couple of years later the politicians decided that the high schools would distribute condoms to students to prevent the spread of STDs. You would think that this would be easy to do. The school nurse could have a supply and students would stop in and be given one on demand. It should be simple. Wrong!

Politicians have to involve lawyers to protect themselves They had to spend school district money on lawyers to make sure that this was legal and that there would not be any repercussions. The lawyers had to find enough "what if's" to justify their fees. They were concerned that the school could be libel if a student did not use the condom correctly. The student could get a disease or get pregnant. Then they would sue the school district.

The school was required to instruct each student on how to use a condom. In this school there were almost three thousand students and about 50 students transferred in or out from other high schools every month. Each student new to the building had to be condom certified. Student privacy was an issue. Accurate records had to be kept. So, handing out condoms became complicated and relatively expensive.

Students who were condom certified could be given condoms each week. There was a room where the lists of condom eligible students were kept and where they would receive their supply. One day of the week was designated "condom day." On that day, we had condoms appearing all over the school. We had inflated condoms and condom water balloons. They were hanging from light fixtures and decorating hallways. After the first month or so the novelty wore off and condom day was without the drama.

—

Politicians always want to be seen protecting the rights of individual citizens (unless it gets in the way of a pet building project or highway). They are usually champions of student rights. They pass laws and make school policy to protect students from unreasonable educators.

All students, by law, have a right to an education. Sounds good but what does it really mean?

When a student arrived late to school, we could not turn the student away. Late has a different meaning to different people. You are thinking that the student was twenty or thirty minutes late and that it would be reasonable to admit the student. What if the student had arrived late every day? We still would have to admit the student. The school day ended at three o'clock. If the student arrived at two o'clock or even at two thirty, we were required to admit the student. If we did not, we were depriving the student of his/her "right to an education." Likewise, the school required teachers to admit students to their classrooms whenever the student showed up. They could talk and hang out with their friends in the hallway for forty of the fifty minutes of a class period and then show up to class. This was disruptive to the classes. When teachers asked about the rights of the other students whose classes were disrupted by arrival of late students, the teachers were told that it was their problem.

Teachers were told that they could discipline students for disruptive behavior. The most common punishment would be an after school detention. We quickly found out that we needed the student's permission to keep the student after school. It seems that the students have the right to leave the school at dismissal time. They have the right to make plans for their after school time and the students could tell us when it was convenient for them to serve a detention.

Students could not be denied admission to the school or class no matter how disruptive their presence was to the school. We had one student who was diagnosed as too violent to be around other students. The student had to be driven to school in a van with a driver and another adult. Then he was placed in a room with a single teacher where he spent the day with one on one instruction. He had the right to a free education and the school district had to provide a program for him.

Another situation that we had to face on a daily basis was the students who were awaiting trial on various charges. These students were out on bail and had not yet been convicted of a crime. Their rights would have been violated if we treated them differently from other students or isolated them in any way. Teachers did not have right to know if they had a student who was charged with violent behavior in their class. Students waiting trial and charged as a juvenile were assured that, if convicted, they would be released at age 21. This gave them carte blanche to act out and threaten and harass other students. They also threaten teachers. They had little to lose at this point.

When a student committed a criminal act in the school, he or she was often transferred to a different high school in the school district. The teachers in the admitting school were never told why the student had been transferred. Teachers always knew teachers in the other high schools. We had one student transferred into our building who had held a loaded gun to a teacher's head in another high school. He was out on bail and in our school. We were never told of the danger.

—

A school text book costs the school between sixty and a hundred and twenty dollars. It is reasonable to provide every student with a text book. We did this early in the school year. The books are numbered. Each student's book number is recorded and the student signs a receipt for that book number. Before long the students have "lost" their books. The lawyers required the school to issue the students another book. We can ask the student to pay for the lost book, but we cannot require any payment. We may not refuse the student a replacement book. This goes on until we run out of books. Our science department in one school alone lost over $10,000 of books every year.

Non-public schools do not have this problem. They are permitted to hold their students responsible for the textbooks, library books and other materials that are issued by the school. Is it any wonder that these schools have a lower operating cost? These schools also are afforded the opportunity to teach something which is almost never taught in the public schools: *responsibility*.

Students who have learned this have less trouble succeeding in college. They also are more likely to get and keep jobs. This makes them less dependent on government and politicians.

—

The school lawyers seem to find ways to expanding students' rights. A case in point is school lockers. The school system buys and installs lockers in schools for students to use to temporary store their coats, lunch, books and school supplies.

In the past the students were issued a combination lock that also opened with a "master" key that open all the lockers within the school. Members of the school staff could and would periodically open and check student lockers. The school staff felt a responsibility to make sure that there was nothing in student lockers what would be a threat to the health and safety of the other students. Staff would open specific lockers when they smelled or if a student were suspected to have contraband in a locker.

Now the lawyers who write the policy and procedures of the schools have decided that the students have a right to privacy includes their school locker. The students now put their own lock on the locker. The school staff can not open lockers without bolt cutters. This alone constitutes a destruction of student property which creates a problem. The results are that students store all sorts of things in their lockers. They know that things locked in their lockers are relatively safe from the adults who are supposed to be running the school.

Students keep drugs, stolen property and weapons in the lockers. Unless someone tells a staff member that something illegal or dangerous is in the locker it will ever be searched. There are no random searches any more. Even when a staff member suspects that there is something illegal in a locker, there is a procedure for opening a student locker.

One day I was looking out of the small window of my classroom door as my students were busy doing a lab exercise. From this corner room I could see the down the hallway and see the students who don't attend class wandering around. I watched two boys open a locker and place a gun in the locker. I did not recognize these students, I only really saw the back of their heads. They locked the locker and left the area. Then I went out into the hallway and got the number of the locker. I called school security from my classroom phone and reported what had occurred.

A few minutes later two school police officers arrived. They checked the locker lock and said that it was locked. Duh.

"Where are your bolt cutters?" I asked.

"We are not allowed to cut locks off of lockers until we first ask the student to open the locker."

Then they went to the student locker list to find the name of the student who had been given this locker for this school year. Next they checked his class roster to locate the student. Of course, he wasn't in his assigned classes. They would not cut the lock and open the locker as I requested. I was told that they had to respect the student's rights. The school policy and procedure had to be followed. In short, it took them three days to actually locate the student and bring him up to unlock the locker. By that time there was no gun in the locker.

Some of us think that this was not in the best interests of the school—wrong! If a gun were recovered it would require a written report. The news media would report the incident and the school's image would be tarnished. It would require an investigation which would take time and money away from other school functions. It was very unlikely that anyone would confess to owning the gun. Even if the students were charged and convicted, they would be put on probation. The most that would happen would be that they would be transferred to another high school in the city. Students on probation are required to attend school or else. Students on probation in this school always had good attendance records. They have the right to attend high school until they are 21 or graduate. Without being on probation, these students will stop attending sooner.

The school's policy and procedures were based on both politics and economics. The school was not operated to satisfy the staff or to the benefit of the students.

—

The city schools first began to screen students for weapons in the late '90s. My district put together groups of school police with hand held metal detectors to screen students. There were over 200 schools in the district. The teams would be randomly assigned a school each day. They would show up about an hour before the school opened. We would arrive to find eight to ten school police cars parked in front of the school. They would set up their screening area about 50 feet inside the main entrance. As the students arrived, they would be scanned individually. This was a slow procedure and soon there would be a line of student out the door and across the parking lot waiting to get into school. It took until the end of the first class period to get all the students screened and in the building.

The school police screeners almost never found a student with a weapon. Teachers would watch from their classroom windows. Many students took a look at the situation and quickly turned around. They went somewhere else for the morning. Later in the day teachers could go outside the building and find a variety of weapons in the bushes around the school.

We had a rash of serious incidents in our school involving some weapons. A group of teachers went to the principal to make the weapon screening more effective. It was suggested that the police cars not be parked in front of the building. The teachers wanted the students to be allowed in the building and sent to the auditorium to sit until they could be screened by the school police.

This shows how naive teachers are about the operation of schools. The school police refused to consider such a procedure. The real purpose of the weapon search was to show the public that the schools were weapon free. A search done as outlined by the teachers would likely result in problems. The school police would actually find students with weapons and would have to deal with the situation. The newspapers or TV would report on the discovery of students with weapons.

It should also be noted that the policy of the school police was not to charge a special educational student found with a weapon. The joke among teachers was that any student with a weapon who stood in line for twenty minutes waiting to be searched would automatically qualify for a special educational classification.

The security procedures in place today (airport-type screening) are really more for show than detection. The school police are armed with walkie talkies. They are not actually prepared to deal with any student with a serious weapon.

Later in the day the students leave and re-enter the building without being screened. Physical education classes go out to the playing fields, often crossing public streets and school parking lots.[44] Some schools still allow the students to leave the building for lunch. My anatomy lab offered the students a collection of scalpels, scissors, knives, probes, etc. The art department, the phys ed department, cafeteria kitchen, and maintenance storeroom also had many pieces of equipment that could be used as weapons. An intelligent student would have no trouble getting a weapon into a school building or finding one already in the building.

—

In tough schools the students get into fights. Students usually don't start fights in classrooms because the teacher can see which student threw the first punch and it gets broken up quickly. Fights usually occur in the hallways. Often these fights are between groups of students. It is usually difficult to sort out the attackers from those who were defending themselves. School laws, codes, and policies make it difficult and costly to expel a student for fighting. There were several fights every week in one high school where I worked. Teachers would break up the fights and the students would be given a three to ten day suspension to cool off. Their parent or guardian was required to meet with the dean before the student was reinstated. The law required the school to reinstate with student within ten days whether or not the parent contacted the school. The students all knew this as did the parents whose children got into trouble regularly.

Almost every month a teacher would get injured breaking up a fight. The teacher could use "sick days" to recover or they could claim "workman's compensation." Our contract allowed teachers to accumulate sick leave and receive a half day's pay for each unused day upon retirement.

44 See Farber's first postulate.

Most teachers brought a long term disability insurance. The cost of this insurance was based on the number of unused sick days that the teacher had accumulated. The teachers who were hurt breaking up a fight were hurt again financially when they took sick days to recover from their injuries.

To claim workman's compensation, the teacher had to go to specific doctors and hospitals. Workman's compensation only paid when the teacher was out more than ten days. It never paid for the first three days, so the teachers always lost three days' pay. Most injuries were strains. A strain or the occasional broken bone would not require a teacher to miss two weeks.

A teacher in the room next to me was body slammed when he attempted to stop two groups from fighting. He suffered four broken ribs and a badly sprained back. He was out on workman's comp for a while. The school was not happy. This teacher received a letter from the school stating that his injuries were his fault. It said that it was not his job to break up fights and he would be terminated if he intervened in another student to student altercation. These situations were to be handled by the non-teaching assistants or school police. One can only imagine the chaos of an inner city school where all the teachers stood by waiting for the arrival of NTAs or school police to break up fights.

Teachers will risk physical harm, break school policy and ultimately risk their jobs to protect students from other students. They will get no support or thanks from school lawyers or politicians.

—

The politicians who ultimately run the schools are interested in having the schools look good to the public. They are unhappy when parents of students complain. They want only positive press about the schools. They reward staff who contribute to the positive image of the schools and punish those who may find fault. It is sometimes not wise to suggest ways to improve a school unless asked. A suggestion to improve may spotlight something which is negative to the school's image.

Some of the people who contribute most to the positive image of a school are the coaches and physical educational staff. They work with parents and alumni to develop support for teams. They raise money for equipment, uniforms and travel expenses to special events such as invitational tournaments or playoffs. They learn early in their careers to always be positive about the school and its programs. Coaches learn how to get good publicity for their teams. They develop contacts with the news media and learn how to give an interview. They are often the best choice for the position of school principal. They can usually be counted on not to try to raise academic standards which would result in lower grades and parent complaints.

The primary job of a school principal is to make sure that the school has a good image. The principal must learn how to handle the press and to "spin" to deflect something which could be negative.

A visitor to the school noticed the bullet holes in some of our large plate glass windows. The principal blamed the holes on the neighborhood. The visitor was told that someone had shot at the building one night. This was a good story and the person did not know that a bullet makes a small entrance hole on one side of the glass and knocks out a larger piece of glass on the exit side. Actually the holes were made by bullets fired from inside of the building.

Another time there was a fight and a student was taken out by ambulance. The principal was interviewed by the press. He said only that there was an "incident" where a student was "punctured." The press did not have the word "stabbed" or "fight" from him thus the school did not get much negative publicity.

Principals and school district administrators never stop trying to spin even the most serious of school incidents. One morning a teacher in the school where I worked was attacked at knife point, tied up and raped in her classroom. The first thing that the principal said publicly was "the rapist was not a student." He quickly had to retreat from this. There were about

2500 students enrolled in the building. The teacher could not identify all of them. He then changed his statement to "the teacher did not recognize the rapist as one of her students.[45]

To put a spin on this, the teachers were told that we would be helped by the district. I suggested that they provide us with self-defense training. Of course that would be logical and is in direct violation of the first postulate of education. By this time school administrators were well aware that I was crazy (second postulate) and could safely ignore my comments.

On our next school day we arrived to find the news media at the school. The school district paraded "rape counselors" into the building. The district "helped" by forcing us to spend the day in rape counseling sessions. What does a rape counselor say to a six-foot-two, 230-pound man who works in one of the toughest schools in the city? If this had been twenty years earlier in my career, I would have caused some problems. By this time I knew that the counseling was not for me. It was only for the school image. It was the politicians putting a spin on a bad situation. They showed that they were "doing something." Counseling is politically correct. It makes this an "isolated' incident rather than the result of a systemic failure that could happen again.

—

In my city a school board member stood up at a meeting and proposed that all students be required to have a year of black history as a requirement for graduation. Since it was a politically correct thing to do, it was passed without any study or input from the district social studies teachers. Suddenly the social studies department had to develop and write a curriculum for this. It had to find and purchase suitable textbooks. This

---

45   To this day the rapist has not been caught. I'm not sure that the powers that be are unhappy about this. There would have been a great deal more bad publicity about the school if the rapist were captured and tried.

additional graduation requirement meant that the students had one less elective course in high school.

This is not the only social studies course imposed by politicians. Many states require a year of "state" history. In many states a course of state history is required by all teachers to receive the state teaching certificate. It is applied equally to math teachers and social studies teachers.

There are at least five states that require a special unit on the holocaust to be included high school social studies. As far as I know, there are no states that require Asian-American history or Hispanic studies in the high school curriculum. I am sure that it is only a matter of time until these will be required.

—

Every parent wants to see their child receive better grades. The politicians oblige them with laws and policies that allow astute parents to get special privileges for their offspring. All they need to do is to get a psychologist to say that their child has some sort of a learning or emotional problem. Then they schedule a conference with a school administer to negotiate a contract to give their child the special conditions needed to compensate for the "learning problem."[46] The lawyers pretty much require school administrators to agree to anything that is recommended by the parents' psychologist.

There are parents who have negotiated for their child unlimited time to take any quiz or test. If a teachers gives a ten minute test or "pop quiz" at the beginning of the period, this child can sit with the quiz for the whole period and into the next period if they so choose.

I had one student who seldom did his homework and was diagnosed

---

46   This was originally directed to students with vision or hearing problems that needed special arrangements to get the same information as the other students. Like many good things, it gets expanded and twisted until it has to be discarded because it no longer helps anyone.

as "homework stressed."[47] This student played electronic games rather than his homework. (Other students in the class told me that they were playing the games with him.) His parents worked out an agreement with the school that he could turn in any and all assignments a week late. We had to accept them for full credit. In reality, I returned assignments and went over them in class by that time.

I asked the vice principal, who had signed the contract, if it was okay if I (and all of his other teachers) turned in this student's grade a week late. She said that I had to turn in grades on time, but could put through a "grade change" when the "week later" school work was turned in to me. While I was tempted to do this, I have learned to pick my fights.[48] I then inquired if the school would hold a special graduation ceremony a week late to allow him to complete his requirements for graduation?

If you think that this only occurs in public schools, you are wrong. In many colleges this is also happening. This is especially true of state colleges and community colleges. These schools are subject to the control of politicians. Parents who have manipulated the public schools for their children are applying the same tactics to the colleges. The so called "helicopter" parents are a new phenomenon for many college professors.

—

There was a time when a new school board or school superintendent could just fire all the teachers and hire friends to replace them. Teachers kept their jobs by supporting politicians. They were expected to make campaign contributions or kick back a part of their salary. They were made to take on

---

47   In the old days this was called either procrastination or laziness. Now it is a "syndrome" thus eligible for special privileges. Next, Medicare or health insurance will pay for treatment.

48   Remember postulate four: "It is better to give than receive, so give everyone a rough time."

many other duties beyond their classroom duties.

Tenure changed all that. No longer did public school teachers serve at the whim of the local politicians? Teachers could only be fired for "just cause." Cause was generally defined by the tenure laws as morals violations or academic incompetence. The school board had to show in court, if necessary, that there was evidence to satisfy "just cause."

Administrative positions do not normally have tenure. In the not too distant past, teachers who wanted to be promoted to principal or vice principal, found promotions were controlled by local politicians. In cities the committeemen or city councilmen had input on staffing on many nonteaching school district positions. Politically astute superintendents would create staff positions for friends of politicians.

At the college and university level, academic freedom comes with tenure. Obtaining tenure in a university can be very difficult.

Today's politicians hate tenure. It has robbed them of the power to fully control the schools. With the legal power of teacher unions behind them, teachers can no longer be forced to do extracurricular jobs without compensation. Tenure is used by politicians as the reason schools fail.

Private and charter schools are not bound by tenure laws. When the board or headmaster changes, there is often a huge turnover of the teaching staff. Many colleges and universities are filling their classrooms with adjunct professors to avoid having a large number of tenured professors. Many of the great universities were run by the tenured professors.

There is the story of General Eisenhower when he became chancellor of Columbia University. He opened a meeting saying "Fellow employees of Columbia University ..." A tenured professor quickly told him that "we are Columbia University."

There are very definite limits to tenure in public institutions. The real problem is that the incumbent on the school administration to demonstrate or prove "just cause." This takes time and work to document. It runs the risk of airing the school's dirty laundry in an open forum when the teacher mounts a defense to the school's charges. No politician wants to open a controversy. They would rather ignore a " problem teacher" as long as possible.

As a union president and a union reprehensive, I have gone to school administrators asking them to start building a case against a problem teacher. My job was to defend the teacher. I always did my job. Unfortunately, school administrators seldom did the work necessary to show "just cause." Too many principals find it easier to write a great recommendation and then get the teacher a job in another school.

—

Teachers and teacher unions are regularly blamed for the high cost of education. The public and politicians conveniently forget that the majority of the employees of most school districts are not teachers. As a pointed out in Chapter 5, my district had 3 non-teaching employees for every 2 teaching employees. Thousands more were indirectly employed by the district via contracts with companies to food service and cleaning services for the district. In the community college where I taught, in a five year period the number of administrators increased by 50% while the number of students and teachers did not change. The teachers will always be blamed for the high cost of education.

—

I saw a tee shirt that said:

"Those who can, teach.
Those who can't,
pass laws about teaching."

It is another way to let people know that education is run by lawyers and politicians, not educators. Teaching is no different than private industry. The captains of industry may have little knowledge of the workings of the products that their factories produce. Anyone who does not like the rules of the job can quit. The school laws, policies and procedures are what they are. There are very few employees in business or industry who can define the parameters of their job. People who complain and gripe only make themselves and the people around them unhappy. Don't fight it. Accept that which you can not change and enjoy your students. Teaching can be a fun and rewarding job. You have a lot to share with your students. You will learn from each other.

CHAPTER 10

Farber's Tenth Postulate

EDUCATION IS THE BLAME / CURE FOR EVERYTHING THAT IS WRONG WITH SOCIETY

This postulate is so very evident that it hardly needs to be discussed. So, this chapter will be short. There is hardly a person among us that has not been in the company of someone who blames the educational system for something. Everyone has spent enough years in school to feel qualified to speak authoritatively about what is wrong with education. Most of the suggested cures will start with the phrase "there ought to be a course …" If all the critics had their way, it would take at least three more years to get out of high school.

This may be the only postulate that is taught in the educational colleges of America. Most teacher training curricula require a course in the history and philosophy of education. This course may start with education in prehistoric or very primitive cultures. The goal of education in even these societies is to orient the individual to the social and physical environment. Society functions well when all members know and follow its rules. Societies prosper when its members are well oriented to their environment.

The next step is to use education to *improve* and *strengthen* a society. This requires the teaching student to study the teachings of the Greek philosophers and founders of the major religions.

One learns that education was used in America to develop economic strength and instill the local religion. By the 1600s many colonies passed laws requiring apprenticeship training of all children. Reading and writing were required so that men could have "the knowledge of the scriptures."[49]

It follows that when people, especially younger people, don't seem to be conforming to the present norms of society that there is something missing in their education. The United States encompasses many different cultures. Each of the original states was established by a group with their own cultural norms. Quickly within the individual states there were sub groups or cultures established. Local control over education is fiercely defended. My state has over 400 individual school boards. Each school board establishes educational policies and curricula requirements that reflect the cultural values of the community. It is said that a society builds its largest buildings for that which the culture most values. In most communities the largest building is a school building. What does this tell us about our society?

When there are economic problems in our country, again the education system can be blamed for not teaching the "right" skills. We live in a dynamic economic society. The skills needed for the job market are changing ever faster. The educational systems are expected to provide the skills necessary for its students to enter the job market. Schools quickly develop courses or programs to meet the expectations.

Many religious groups founded colleges in the 1800s. The underlying purpose of these schools was to instill the values of the particular religious denomination. These liberal arts colleges produced teachers, preachers, lawyers, etc. The roots of many of our colleges and universities to day go back to this movement. They were not focused on engineering or technical skills.

Back in the civil war days congress was concerned about people having the skills to expand the nation beyond the Mississippi river. There was much to be built to tame the West. The Morrill Land Grand of 1862 encouraged each state to establish a university. The purpose of these universities was to teach agriculture, engineering, science and the classics. Notice

---

49   From the "Old Deluder Staten Law" establishing schools in the Massachusetts Bay Colony in 1647.

the order and thus the importance. These schools were expected to produce graduates with the skills to conquer the west. These were people who would find a way to make the new lands productive. These were the people who would build the infrastructure of roads, bridges, railroads, communications, etc. that would tie the distant lands with the rest of the nation. The job was almost completed within a generation. By 1900 there was no longer a frontier.

America had a new problem. Masses of immigrants were arriving daily. They were needed by the still young and growing nation. In cities they formed communities of their own. The leaders of the nation realized the immigrants needed to be "Americanized." The educational system provided the means to do this. The primary purpose of public schools was to teach the immigrants' children to be good productive citizens of the United States. All classes were taught in English and so everyone could communicate with all other citizens. They were taught the history and values of the young nation. They believed in the "melting pot" concept of the nation. The products of these schools identified themselves first as Americans.

The next major problem of the nation was economic. The great depression began and the job market collapsed. The schools could not teach any skill that would result in a job for a young person. The educational system could not create jobs. Young men (or boys) would work cheaper and were often stronger than older workers. Education was used to protect the dwindling number of jobs from the competition of youth. Compulsory education laws were passed in state after state to keep the youth in school and out of the job market as long as possible. Child labor laws were passed to punish employers who knowingly hire youth who should have been attending school.

Control of disease in the nation became possible by the development of vaccines Schools are a place where infectious diseases can be passed from child to child. It also became the place to fight the spread. Children were required to have numerous vaccinations before being admitted to school. Children are required by law to attend school therefore all children are required by law to be vaccinated. The educational system was used to cure the population of infectious disease.

Before World War II, colleges were elitist institutions. The majority of students came from upper class families. The GI bill changed this. A college education became possible for veterans. It provided an alternative for returning soldiers and sailors who did not have good civilian jobs waiting for them. College classrooms were filled with battle hardened war veterans who wanted to take part in the post war economic boom. They were more serious students, in a hurry to get on with their lives and careers. The fact that most of these men went on to successful careers changed the American perspective of a college education. It was now considered a key to success in American society. It became a prerequisite to upward mobility in major corporations.

Then sputnik appeared in 1957. Americans were shocked by the appearance of the Russian moon. We had fallen behind the Soviets in science and technology. Immediately the educational system was blamed. The schools should steer more students into science, math and engineering. The schools should require more rigorous courses in science and math. No one seemed to notice that the government really had not funded a major program to develop satellites. The program was a minor footnote on a navy rocket development project. The schools and educators received all the blame. The cure for this national embarrassment would be to change the educational system.

The science and math courses were said to be out of date. Their curriculums had to be more than revised. Nationally funded groups were formed to completely re-write all science and math courses. Science and math teachers were sent to federally funded summer institutes to be retrained. Schools were required to build more science laboratories. Students were require to take more science and math courses. School schedules were revised to give the students more time in science laboratories. Grant money became readily available for teachers of math and science, even on a middle or elementary school level.

Then, when it became evident that America would win the race to the moon, the money for new science and math programs dried up. Schools gradually reduced funds for science lab equipment and supplies.

The next national problem was racial prejudice and discrimination. Once again the educational system was both a big part of the problem and the solution. Many schools were racially segregated. Schools were required to be racially integrated. Complex bussing programs, over seen by federal judges, were imposed on school districts all over the nation. Colleges and universities were required to have racially integrated student bodies.

On the heels of the national need to solve the problems created by racial prejudice came the need to allow women full access to careers in all aspects of business and industry. Educators were especially blamed for not encouraging more girls to pursue careers in math, science and engineering. Educators took on the responsibility to cure the situation. Schools developed programs for women in science and engineering. Math and science courses were revised to make them more female friendly.

When cars became more available to teenagers, the number and rate of teenage automobile accidents increased. The schools (not parents) were soon given the responsibility of training young people to drive automobiles. Driver education became an integral part in most suburban high schools.

After teaching students how to drive, we discovered that American students were not as physically fit as students in other countries. Again, the education system was blamed. Physical fitness programs became a part of the school curriculum.

As the rate of teenage pregnancy increased, it became a problem of the schools. The solution was to have more and earlier sex education in the schools.

The same can be said for the problem of drugs in our society. The educational system is expected to provide a drug education program to prevent students from using drugs.

It was determined that American children tend to be overweight. This

is not healthy. Yet again, the schools were blamed. In my day, school cafeteria food was not that good. Schools responded to complaints about the
food and made the food more appetizing. Now the students were eating
too much. The cure was to eliminate the foods that the students really liked
and replace it with more salads and veggies.

Most recently we have discovered that people are bullied. The schools
are supposed to cure society of this problem by the development of anti-
bullying programs.

About the only thing that the schools haven't been blamed for is students not getting enough sleep. It may be the next thing that will be blamed
on the schools. Then teachers will be sent to in-service workshops to learn
how to deliver super-dull lessons.

—

There are some people who believe that the schools shouldn't be called
upon to solve all of society's ills. They think that educators should just say
"no." These are the problems of the students home or they are problems of
society at large rather than school problems.

There are two problems with the idea of saying "no."

First thing is that educators don't run the schools. They are employees
of the school system. They must follow the mandates of the school system if they want to keep their jobs. Politicians decide what the schools will
teach or not teach. The educators are simply told that they need to find a
way of providing a program to solve whatever problem that our leaders
think needs a cure.

Second is the fact that with every "new" problem comes money to develop a cure. School curriculum is driven by money. No school administrator will remain in his/her job long if they turn away money that is available
to the school.

CHAPTER 11

Farber's Eleventh Postulate

EDUCATION IS THE ONLY BUSINESS WHERE THE CUSTOMER IS SATISFIED WITH LESS AND LESS PRODUCT

The consumers of education are the students and their parents. The product of education is assumed to be knowledge and cognitive skills obtained by the student. Most people assume that a student's grades are a result of a measurement of the amount of knowledge and skills that the student has gained in a particular subject.

To understand this postulate we need to think about several different components of the education system:

1. The need to please the consumer.
2. The packaging of the institution's image.
3. The graduation requirements.
4. The knowledge, skills, or attendance time that are required to pass each level or course.
5. The methods of measurement of these skills and knowledge.
6. The attitude of the educational institution toward quality control.

Many of us have heard or used the acronym "NIMBY." It means "not in my back yard." Whenever we have a need for a highway, disposal facility, factory, halfway house, etc., people who otherwise would agree that this thing is needed for the betterment of society suddenly object to it being located in their town or neighborhood. People voice the need for "higher standards" in educational institutions. Wanting higher standards in education is analogous to people wanting to go to heaven. Everyone wants to go to heaven but nobody wants to die. Our chances of going to heaven are far greater than the our chances of raising standards in education. This is because everyone will eventually die. We have no choice. To believe that "eventually" educational standards will be raised is overly optimistic. The consumers or directors of schools have a choice to raise or not raise educational standards. The consumers of education will not choose to impose higher standards on themselves or their children. They only want higher standards are only be applied to someone else. School boards and trustees know that if they impose higher standards, they will face consumer complaints and lose customers. It is not a wise way of doing business.

In my over four decades of teaching I have never heard of a teacher being reprimanded for passing too many students or giving too many A's. School boards and administrators know what the consumer wants good grades and high graduation rates. Meeting these criteria (of students earning good grades and raising graduation rates) will get them promoted, re-appointed, or reelected. In education today, no student is considered unable to succeed in anything that the student or parents desire.[50] An eleventh grade student who is 5' 5" is told that if he works hard, he can play in the NBA. Teachers are prohibited from uttering such words as "dumb," "stupid" or "retarded." We are still allowed to use the word "challenged" but that may change. We tell every high school student they should be going to college, even the C-students who come from poor families.[51] Vo-tech

---

50 *Ironically* most schools claim to be preparing students for the "real world."

51 Have you looked at the cost of college recently? Educators wonder why so many poor students drop out of high school. They may be smarter than we think because they realize that if they can't earn a scholarship, they are not likely going to college. They realize that they need to figure out how to make a living.

schools are under siege as not needed in public education today.[52]

—

Schools work very hard to satisfy their customers. They use both a carrot and stick to get teachers to do their bidding. Principals and headmasters can change any grades that are given by teachers but this creates internal conflict in a school. It is better when they can convince a teacher to give higher grades. College and university administrators can not change a professor's grade. Most colleges have a grade appeal process which can make it uncomfortable for professors who use a more subjective grading system. Teachers learn quickly to develop an objective grading system that is written out and clearly presented to students at the beginning of a course. Then good record keeping is essential. All teachers must always be prepared to defend the grades given students.

One spring my school suggested that I should sign up for a summer workshop on "Alternative Grading." This was a two or three week workshop for which the district paid teachers to attend. It turned out that most of the teachers in the workshop were science and math teachers. These required courses often have higher failure rates. (Foreign languages also have higher failure rates but are not required of all students) Science and math teachers are harder to hire and retain, because they often can earn higher salaries in business and industry. This makes them a bit more independent. They tend to grade a bit more objectively and expect their students to actually know something.

The workshop leaders started out the first day talking about how we all think and learn differently. They then went on (and on) about how each

52 Vo-tech schools are many times more expensive. This is the hidden agenda in trying to close these programs. It is relatively cheap to provide a teacher and thirty some seats in a room. The teacher-student ratio in vo-tech should be no more than 1 to 15 for safety reasons. Each area needs many different pieces of very expensive equipment and the program will consume a lot in materials.

individual has different strengths and weakness. Not everyone is good at math or writes well or is good at multiple choice tests. Many people are just not good test takers, but everyone had something where they are strong. We were told that it was not fair to evaluate all students by the same "instrument"(yardstick). We should use different methods of evaluation(grading), based on the student's strengths, for each of the students in our class.

This multiple methods of grading in the same classroom will only work if all of the students receive A's and B's—well, maybe not B's. When a student is given a D or F grade all heck will break loose. But we all knew that the purpose of the workshop was to give these teachers rational to pass all students with good grades. Since we were paid to attend this indoctrination, we went along with it, hoping to get a few usable ideas that could help our students.

The first set of alternative grading schemes involved students producing posters, scrapbooks or collages instead of passing written tests. We were warned that teachers needed to provide magazines, etc. otherwise some students will cut pictures out of textbooks and library books. The point was that a student may not be able to solve a quadratic equation problem, but by making a collage, they show an appreciation of it. We were shown examples of collages and even had a couple of students present and explain their collages to us. Even the students had trouble keeping a straight face when they did their presentations. Think Alice in Wonderland.

Then we were divided into small groups, given a topic, paste, scissors and some magazines, and told to spend the afternoon making collages. These would be presented the next morning. This was a roomful of teachers with earned masters and doctorate degrees from major universities. Why is it that people think that teachers are so dumb. Teachers are just nice, polite people who, too often, allow others to take advantage of them.

The next set of alternate grading ideas involved the students doing poems, raps, skits, etc. instead of displaying a knowledge of the subject on tests. Considering my lack of appreciation of current teen music and rap, this alternative grading would not have been much benefit to my students. Maybe next summer the district would send me to a rap music appreciation workshop.

Finally the workshop leaders got to the old favorite—group work. They told us that "scientific studies" show that students do better(higher grades) when they work in groups. Students should do projects, reports, labs and even take tests as a group. The group, not the individual would receive a grade, thus everyone in the group would get the same grade. We were told to assign students to groups so that each group had the same number of A, B, C, D, and F students. Of course we all know that the more motivated students in the group would do all the work and learning. The unmotivated students would be carried by others. If any group failed, the groups would be broken up and reconstituted.

At this pointing the workshop, I was having difficulty keeping quiet. I pointed out that a class is, in reality, a group. The group grading logic could just as easily be applied to the class and I could give everyone the same grade which would be the class average. Of course, logic does not apply in education.

In my classes we do lab work in pairs or groups depending on the complexity of the lab and the equipment available. I explain(warn) at the beginning of year that anyone who does not contribute to the success of the group will soon find that others will not want him/her in their group. The workshop leaders told me that this was the wrong approach.

I suggested what I thought was a better way of using groups in the class. I would empower the students(educational buzzword) in the process of forming groups. My method would be cross curricular(another buzzword) as well. I would let the students vote on the method of forming groups. The students would get a lesson in 'problems of democracy" in science class. They would choose between:

1. Teacher forming groups with the same number of A, B, C, etc. students in each group; or

2. Teachers forming their own groups but with the condition that each group with a passing group grade would be taxed (have a 2–3 points deducted from their grade) and these points given to lower performing groups so that they have a passing grade.

I thought that this was a great idea. They told me that it was a terrible idea. No way should such a thing be done in a classroom. They came up with a list of things that were wrong. I concluded that there were no practicing liberals in educational administration.

In my experience, most science teachers allow students to choose their lab partners or group. As chairman of a large science department, I regularly received complaints from parents concerning this. They would tell me that their child was grouped with someone who did not work. They wanted me to force the teacher to place their child in a high performing group. I would explain that we allowed students to make their own choices. I would then go on that learning to make good choices was actually more important that learning science.[53] They needed to learn to pick good friends and they needed to exhibit traits that would allow them to associate with the people with whom they wanted to be. We are trying to prepare students for the real world.

I know what you are thinking. "If you can't blind them with brilliance, baffle them with B.S." Not so. I really believe that teaching students to make good choices is very important. You can help them learn from their poor choices as well as their good ones.

Universally students would like to receive, if not A's, at least passing grades. They all want to graduate from their schools. Their parents want the same thing. Parents do not call a teacher to complain about a student receiving a high grade or about the lack of failing grades. College students

---

53   One had to be careful when telling this to a single divorced parent. Always do this in person of or the phone. Never use emails. They will come back to haunt you.

will not file a grade grievance if they learned nothing in a course while receiving an A grade. No one will ask to see that teacher's grade book, course outline, or to in any way justify the grades. Let a teacher give a failing grade to a student, and he or she will most certainly hear from someone. In fact, teachers' grades are closely monitored by administrators. In most schools, the administrators receive a printout of each teacher, class by class, which highlights the number and percentage of failures in each class. The teachers with "above average" number of failures are often called in to explain or defend the number of failures. The fact that some tenured teachers may not be intimidated by this is one of the main objections to the practice of awarding tenure. Many private and charter schools do not award tenure. This allows them better control over the grades awarded by teachers and thus makes them more attractive to parents and students. Teachers who have low failure rates are more likely to be offered administrative positions. They obviously understand the system better and therefore are more able to operate it smoothly.

This brings us to the image of the educational institution. How does a school build a positive image while trying to please the consumer with minimal product? Colleges and universities want to have the reputation of preparing their graduates for success in their chosen fields. They would like to point to graduates who are successful. This is not always easy. Often graduates take advanced degrees at other schools. The problem is which school should get credit for the success of this person. Another problem is that it takes a decade or two of working in the "real" world for the success of a person to be recognized. This time lag creates a variety of problems, especially for lesser known schools and schools which are expanding and changing.

For a school to have graduates that are truly superior it must be able to do one of two things. It can limit admissions to only well prepared students or flunk out students who do not perform well.

Colleges can limit admission to only those who have outstanding SAT or ACT test scores and great high school records or it can flunk out all the students who can not perform at high levels. There are a few schools that have a reputation of having several hundred applicants for every place in their freshman class. They can actually choose only the brightest and best. They can also charge truly outrageous tuition. But even these schools must accept some less qualified students in order to fund brilliant scholarship students. Almost all schools set aside some places for "legacy" students. These are the sons and daughters of the rich and powerful, particularly alumni. These students serve several purposes. Their families fund building projects and endowments. Their presence allows the other students to establish useful contacts which results in the networking of graduates who help each other rise faster in their professions.

At the other end of the scale are the community colleges. By law they usually have to accept almost any graduate of the local high schools. They typically have two year programs. After successful completion of this program, the student can transfer his or her credits to a four year college and enter as a junior. The community college is far less costly to attend than a four year college. The four year colleges really don't want to lose out on two years tuition with all these students. They look for ways not to accept all the credits that a student earned at the community college. This in turn puts pressure on the community college not to pass students who have not learned the material. The community college will accept a high course failure rate in order to ensure that course credits are accepted by the four year colleges.

It can take decades of screening admissions and/or flunking out poor students for a school to gain a reputation of excellence. It is easier and quicker to purchase a reputation. This can be done without the hassle of flunking students or denying admission to students whose families can afford the tuition.

It is possible to purchase a reputation by hiring teachers known for their accomplishments. Universities hire well know experts, researchers, and authors. These people may not actually teach many classes, instead they will do research and supervise the work of graduate students. They are useful to the university only as long as they are recognized for their work in their area. They must be presenting papers at conferences while representing the university. This has led to the typical university atmosphere of "publish or perish." Schools with enough capital can even hire Noble Laureates. The university calls upon them to meet with certain visiting groups and give a talk which usually involves a slide show of their receiving the Noble prize.

Public schools can also do this. They can require teachers to have advanced degrees. The parents can see the academic credentials of a school's teachers on line, in the school catalogue, or in the school yearbook. Most schools now require a person to have a masters' degree to supervise a kindergarten classroom.[54]

Schools want to have a reputation for quality and high standards. Schools with high graduation rates are considered "good schools" while a school that has a low rate of graduation is called "a troubled school," "a problem school," or just plain "a school that is failing."

Webster's defines "*standard*" to be something that constitutes or affords a comparison or judgment. In common usage the word implies that some sort of uniform and well established gauge is applied to measure the quality of the product.

There are countless government agencies, bureaus, regulators, etc., that write standards for everything that we make, buy, sell or dispose of in our trash. The complexity of a product has never been a deterrent to the government standard writers. They have managed to find a way to write standards for everything from paper clips to airplanes. There is actually a standard for the number of rat hairs that are permitted in a can of beans. Some of these standards are so detailed that we need to hire specialists to help us adhere to at least the minimum acceptable standards.

The requirements for high school graduation vary from state to state. Within any particular state the individual school districts are usually

---

54   And now the public wonders why the cost of public education is high.

permitted to add their own criteria to the state requirements, which are usually called the minimum requirements for high school graduation. Is it therefore *logical* to assume that there are some minimum standards for high school graduation in every public and private school licensed by the state? Here you are reading the last of Farber's postulates and still are not fully following the first. You were tripped up by applying logic to education again. In the *real* world of education, it never applies.

The first thing that most people assume is that there are standards in American education. This is an incorrect assumption. There are no standards. The term standard implies that there is some uniform measurement that is applied to all students. This could be all students in a particular state, a specific school district, an individual school with in a district or a grade level within a school. The reality is that this has never existed longer than it takes for an influential parent[55] to complain or for the cost of operating a school to go up by a few thousand dollars.

Many members of the public are under the mistaken belief that there is some sort of a minimum educational or skill level standard for graduation from high school. If such a standard requirement for graduation from a high school existed, it would be some *measurable skill* or *testable body of knowledge* that every graduating student must have in order to receive a diploma. If you say that you have a standard, but you can't define it, measure it, or test it, *then it does not really exist.*

Ask your school to tell you exactly what is required of a student for high school graduation. Most schools have a list of credits or courses that a student must "pass" in order to graduate. This is the traditional way that most states and colleges issue as a criterion for a diploma. The list of courses may have changed from time to time to reflect the current "crisis" in education. (*Everything that actually causes any change in education is a crisis; Le Chatelier's principle prevents anything less from being noticed beyond*

---

55   There are no criteria to qualify as a parent. They are not required to demonstrate any knowledge of child rearing or even the ability to read or write.

the confines of the school house.) When math scores are down, the state requires an additional credit of math When social unrest is a problem, another course in social studies is included. The opposite happens when the drop out percentage is too high, the number of math credits is reduced and the list of optional credits accepted toward graduation is increased. These optional credits might include courses in folk lore, indoor horticulture, job search, science fiction movies etc.

Well, this course credit system may not be the system that suits everyone, but it is usually acceptable to most people. It seems to spell out a minimum that a student must learn in order to earn a diploma in the particular state. This sounds good or is acceptable to enough people.

Let's look a bit closer at this system.

First we must ask what constitutes a *course*. While this varies somewhat from state to state, there are usually no real major differences in the definition of a course. The state or school usually has something that boils down to a statement that a course has a written syllabus and consists of so many hours of instruction (usually about 120 hours for a high school course) This usually is quite close to the requirements put forth by the Carnegie unit.

Now look a little closer. How many hours is the student required to be present in class for this instruction. Now it gets a bit more interesting. Most schools have no absolute requirements for students actual attendance in a specific course. The list of reasons that a student may be *excused* from being in class seems endless. There is no statement of the minimum percentage of the instructional hours that a student is permitted to miss and still be given credit. When a student is not in class how can the instructional time be made up? Again there is no statement that addresses this point. A teacher seeking guidance from a building principal will hear words like "reasonable" or "comparable." Try to get agreement on what is "reasonable." All sides in any dispute will tell you that *they* are being reasonable but the other side is *un*reasonable. I've been in labor negotiations where both sides sincerely believed that they were being reasonable and yet they were worlds apart. Again the word *comparable* is a matter of your point of view.

At this point we are talking about "excused absences." What about un-excused absences or simply nonattendance of instructional periods. Most college courses have a policy or statement on "cuts." There is usually a grade reduction associated with cuts. So after a certain number of cuts it is not possible to receive a passing grade in the course. This is not true of high schools and grade schools. Students, by law, are required to attend school, therefore there should be no unexcused absences. Like most laws, it is only as good as its enforcement.

So what is the bottom line when it comes to attendance? My experience is that there is no bottom line. I have seen students who were absent more than 80% of the school year not only passed to the next grade, but were graduated from high school that year. Teachers often see students at gradu-ation that they haven't seen in their class for months. It is amazing that the schools will graduate people who barely even attended. It is probably cheaper to graduate them that to pay to maintain the empty space in the classrooms that would be needed for them if these students were held back since these non-attending students would continue not to occupy the classroom.[56]

A couple of states have passed a minimum school attendance require-ment for promotion, but I know of no state that has a minimum course at-tendance requirement. In many urban school districts the school building is a hang out or social center. There are many students who attend school regularly but do not attend classes. They go to the advisory or homeroom period where the *official* school attendance is taken. This keeps them on the official roll and prevents the school from calling their home to inquire about why they are not in school. These kids then hang out in hallways, lunchrooms, lavatories, or the school yard. These kids have dropped out of education, but they have not dropped out of school. If the schools made them go to classes, they might drop out of school. This would increase the

------

56   See Chapter 7.

dropout rate of the high school and look bad on the district's statistical report ... This is bad for the image of the district. The urban schools have all kinds of programs to keep kids in school. Allowing the school to be a hangout is certainly the most effective way and least costly way to keep the kids on the official roll. It doesn't do much to educate the pupil, but it goes a long was to fulfill the primary purpose of the public school: *public daycare!*

In taking this idea to its fullest development, there are some communities that want to turn the school building into a one stop community service center. This allows the buildings to be used year round. It spreads out the operating cost of the building between the school district and the community services department. They want to locate the public health services, social services office, and legal aid office in the public high school building.[57] In school where I taught, included an infant day care center and a full time state parole officer. I don't know why they did not also include the police department and city jail as part of the school.

Whenever someone talks about minimum attendance requirements for passing a grade or course, school officials[58] begin to talk about the need to emphasize learning over just *putting in the time.* They will make a seemingly convincing argument for giving credit for knowledge and skills rather than just attendance in some "dull" course.

Then you need to ask what is the knowledge or skill that the student is *required* to demonstrate to pass each of these courses. Ask what specific *test* or *skill demonstration* is required to pass each course. In other words, exactly how is this knowledge or skill to be measured to determine if the individual student has a sufficient amount to go on the next level or grade? I know of no school that has an objective measurement of skills or

---

57   This is the Walmart concept of schools. Walmart will provide everything from car service to pharmacy and vision care in one building. Schools may some day adopt the same business plan.

58   These are the same administrators who may require a different teacher to pass a student based on good attendance.

knowledge that determines whether or not a student is given a passing grade for the course. Schools will present all kinds of grading guidelines that teachers are to use but none of these constitutes any sort of uniform standard of knowledge or skill. It is up to each individual teacher to set the minimum standard for his or her course. It is seldom that a teacher is reprimanded or even criticized by school officials for passing students who have little or no knowledge or skill in the subject. Just let a teacher set a high standard for passing his or her subject, and see what happens. It will not take long before the vice principal or principal calls the teacher in for a conference. The teacher will have to defend his or her standards against the school administration. The teacher's grade book and records will be carefully examined for errors. Often the teacher will be asked for copies of tests or exams and these will be examined to determine if the questions are clearly stated and "reasonable." In most cases the teacher will get a clear message that it is better to lower standards and pass students on than to continuously have to defend a standard.

The bottom line here is that the school's courses have no actual standards but the requirements for passing the course changes with each individual teacher. Thus, it would appear that the sum of the individual teachers' requirements add up to the school district's standard. This is not actually the case either. Most school districts and states allow a principal or vice principal to change the grade or grades of any student without consulting the student's teacher or teachers. Almost every year teachers in many school districts are surprised at graduation when they watch a student graduate who has failed one or more courses that the school district *requires* for graduation.

Every couple of years we see and hear of school superintendents or school boards who are telling us how they are going to raise the standard of education. They give long involved talks about all the things that will be done in their district to raise the standards. They wave thick reports and other documents that they claim will set and enforce higher standards for their district.

Think of an astronaut lifting weights in space. The astronaut goes through all the appropriate motions and the weights look real and they sound real The astronaut may have a sly grin on his face as he is doing the weight lifting in space because there is no weight in space. You can't lift weight where none exists. The same is true of standards in education. You can't raise standards if they don't exist in the first place. In all my years as both a student and as a teacher, I have not found even one absolute standard that applies to all students.

Try to determine if there is just one thing all students must be able to do, or to know, or to have demonstrated in order to move to the next grade even to graduate from high school. We have found reason to graduate students who can not do long division, do not know the time tables or can not add simple numbers successfully. We graduate students who can not locate nations on the correct continent on a world map or locate the states on a United States map. We have graduated students who can't write a complete sentence or recognize when a sentence is incomplete, and who can't read the words in a newspaper. There was a time when I thought that all students could tell time, especially quitting time. Then I found a student who could not tell time on a non-digital clock. We can't even honestly call the high school diploma a certificate of attendance since this is not a requirement. And yes we have even given high school diplomas to dead students. No, I have not found one thing that is an absolute requirement to graduate from high school.

Standards of education are truly an illusion. Raising educational standards is truly like lifting weights in space.

—

Every so often there is a "public" outcry for higher standards in our public schools. This is usually brought on by some survey or report of the state of education in America. This occurs once a decade like clockwork. After much discussion about what is wrong with education, some political body or agency decides to correct the situation. The solution that this group will invariably come up with is to have *better teachers*. They ignore the fact that elected school boards hire, evaluate and tenure teachers either directly or through their appointed agents. It is easy to blame teacher unions or tenure laws. It never occurs to such groups that if schools wanted to be able to select teachers from a larger pool of qualified college graduates, schools would need to vastly improve salaries and working conditions. This would attract more people into education. All of this is logical and, therefore, violates Farber's first postulate and must be ignored. The political body appoints a study committee to recommend changes that will improve the educational system, starting with the teachers. This group invariably recommends, and the state requires, as a result, all the teachers to be tested or to go back to college for another course or two. This may appear to be reasonable approach to improving education, at least on the surface.

Let us take a closer look at this approach. Suppose that General Motors took this approach to improving the quality of their cars. Everyone working on the automobile assembly line would be required to pass a written test on the foot-pounds of torque specified for each nut or bolt installed in their phase of the assembly of a car. Does this improve the quality of the car? Not in the least! All of the workers already know what they are *supposed* to do. The problem is doing it. If the production line is moving too fast for them to properly tighten bolts, then there will be loose bolts. If they are not allowed to hold up a faulty unit and fix it, then loose bolts will continue down the line and out the door. If there is not an independent quality control check at each phase of the production, there will be poor quality cars produced. GM doesn't wait until the car is completely assembled and ready to be shipped to do a quality control inspection. General Motors managers know quality control means that they check and test each component of their car. As they build the car, they check each major phase of the vehicle assembly. They don't rely on the person responsible for tightening the bolts to do the quality inspection on these same bolts. They know that quality control personnel must be separate in the corporate structure or chain of command from those concerned with production quotas. GM officials know that there is a profit in producing a car of a specific quality level. They design their production procedures to reach this predetermined quality level.

Schools on the other hand, do not feel it is necessary to check or test any phase of a student's education. Students are not required to exhibit a basic reading skill or math skill to be moved to the next phase or level of education. The school expects the individual teacher to set the quality standard, do the work with the student to reach the standard, test the students against this standard, hold back any students who have not reached the standard, and then the school officials will criticize and even dismiss a teacher who holds back more than one or two students per year. Teachers who never hold back students often are held up as examples of "good" teachers and given choice assignments. There is no incentive for the teacher hold back a student who is not ready for the next level. Likewise, there is no "profit" for the school in producing good students or graduates. It costs about $10,000 to hold one student back one year. This is a loss that increases the cost of education to the taxpayer. In fact there is an incentive for a school district to move students through to graduation as fast as possible: money. The teachers who insist in holding students to some sort of a standard are a hindrance to the financial well-being of the public school district.

GM has an unhappy customer when a car leaves the plant with loose bolts or parts missing. They have to face the wrath of that customer. Schools, on the other hand do not get customer complaints when they graduate students who are deficient in knowledge or skills. Educators only get complaints when they refuse to graduate the customers who don't measure up.

—

Another approach often suggested by politically appointed committees is to reward or punish teachers through a system of "merit pay." On the surface this may sound like an effective way of getting teachers to improve their skills.. Ineffective teachers would change their ways and become more effective teachers in order to earn larger pay raises.

However, let's take a look at reality. Just think back to when you were a student. Everyone has had one or more ineffective teachers. These teachers were immediately punished by their students. The students were restless, inattentive, and soon became disobedient and unruly. This teacher was more physically and emotionally punished by the students than by anything the school board could legally impose. Many such teachers would have willingly given up a pay raise to be able to control and interest the classes. I know of no teacher who is purposefully ineffective. All teachers want to be effective. It makes their day to day life more pleasant and rewarding.

Many people believe that merit raises for teachers would improve the performance of the educational system. It is one of those things which sounds reasonable until it is put into practice. However, merit raises are more likely to work against the overall effectiveness of a school.

Let me give you an example. I had the experience of working in a school that instituted a system of merit raises. At first it seemed like a good idea. The teachers would no longer get small "step" raises based on the years of service. It seemed to be a way for harder working teachers to increase their pay. Then the reality of Farber's seventh postulate set in. There was a budget for merit increases. Only a percentage of the staff could receive a merit raise. Teachers with ten or more years could not easily get another teaching position so they could forget about merit raises. The younger teachers could more easily get a job in another school. Science and math teachers were more in demand. There was a surplus of English and social studies teachers. There were not any clear cut criteria for earning a merit pay increase. It could be based on the grades earned by the students, on the extracurricular school activities sponsored by the teacher, the appearance of the classroom, how well the teacher got along with the principal, etc.

As a result, the merit raises ended up working against the morale of the staff. All teachers were not given equal consideration. Teachers who must compete with each other for raises are less likely to help each other. They are not going to share innovative teaching ideas, share equipment or help other teachers with problems. The team work of the school faculty will disintegrate in a short time and it will become a less pleasant place to work and learn.

—

Some schools and school districts seem to make great improvement in a short span of time. I know of one school district that raised the average SAT scores tremendously in just one year. This sounds like the district raised its standards of education effectively. An inside look told a different story. What really happened is that the high school counselors gave SAT test application forms only to the better students. Poor students were told where to write to get the SAT test application forms. It was inevitable that fewer of the students who would most likely have lower scores took the test that year. Naturally, with the elimination of many of the lower scores, the district average would be much higher. This is just an example of how raising standards is like lifting weights in space. In most cases, when a school district claims to have raised its standards, if you look closely, you will find it is an illusion.

Private schools acquire the reputation of being better schools much the same way. They do not admit students who are slower learners. They also encourage the parents to withdraw children who may be scoring lower on standardized tests. Such actions are not educational standards. They are just ways of keeping average scores high but usually when you look closely, you will find that there are *exceptions* to both admission and retention standards. They just have a larger number of high achieving students in which to hide the non-achievers.

Colleges, too can produce some misleading statistics. Colleges always publish the average SAT scores of their freshman class. How they calculate this average can be interesting. Often a student takes the SAT tests several times. The college will report the highest math scores and the highest verbal of the several attempts of each of the incoming freshman. Many colleges report the SAT scores of the students that the college *accepted* rather than the scores of the students who actually enrolled in the freshman class. Another trick is to omit the SAT scores of all students accepted after the *official* final acceptance date. Usually a sizable number of students are accepted after this date as the college fills the spots vacated by students who were accepted at several schools and have now decided on another school. The result of this is that often the SAT scores of the bottom quarter of freshman attending some schools are not included in the calculation of the freshman SAT average.

—

People, business people in particular, have realized that the high school diploma is about as worthless as a politician's promise. Employers don't even give students a raise when they complete high school.[59] This resulted in some efforts to shore up the image of high school degree.

"No Child Left Behind" was an attempt to set up standards in education for grade promotion and high school graduation. Before the ink was dry on the program, educators were finding ways to exempt students from any possible requirements.[60] Many private schools were exempted from the regulations since they did not receive tax money. "Special" students were not required to pass the standardized tests for promotion. Of course, any student who did not pass could be re-classified as a special student. Then some schools invented the idea of "non-graded" students. A fourth grade student who did not pass the promotion test for fifth grade was reclassified

---

59   What if minimum wage was different for those where high school graduates? This would be the best "stay in school" program ever and would not cost taxpayers anything. It can't happen because it violates Farber's first postulate.

60   See Chapter 6, Le Chatelier's Principle.

a "non-graded" student. This student was not promoted to fifth grade but was not required to repeat the fourth grade. The next year the student sat in a fifth grade classroom with fifth grade students and did fifth grade work. The student was not "officially" a fifth grade student nor was his/her ego hurt by being classified as a fourth grade student. The theory was that this student would eventually catch up. With group learning, the student would likely get passing subject grades.

—

"No Child Left Behind" has raised some very interesting questions about the purposes of schools and what a student ought to know or be able to do at specific levels of education. It is doubtful that educators will ever reach any agreement on these things. Even if all educators could agree on specific standards for promotion and graduation, the politicians who run the schools would not allow implementation of real standards. Politicians could not take the heat that they would get from parents and parent groups when all students are held to the same absolute academic standard.

Any quality control in education is the result of dedicated tenured teachers standing strong against the market pressures for less quality in the product of the schools.

CHAPTER 12

Farber's Twelfth Postulate

TEACHERS CAN'T BE PROMOTED; THEY ALREADY HAVE THE BEST JOB IN EDUCATION

You graduate from college with a degree in education and you get your first teaching job. The school year begins and you enter your classroom to face some thirty odd students. You have begun your teaching career. If you are good, really good, you will still be in a classroom with some thirty odd students thirty five or forty years from now, and enjoying it. It may become hard to give up this job and retire.

Like many things in education, the career ladder is a bit backwards. You get to start with the best job in the industry. It is not only the most fun but also the most important job. The interface between the classroom teachers and students is where learning occurs. The teachers do most of the counseling. The teachers are the primary disciplinarians. The teachers set the learning expectations and the grading standards.

Because you have the best job in the educational industry, you are relieved of the normal competition for promotion to a better job. This gives you a remarkable degree of freedom and independence. You can focus on doing that which is best for your students. Within limits, you don't have to jump on every educational bandwagon that comes down the road. You can pick and choose to serve school committees that are relevant to your teaching. You can concentrate on honing your teaching skills and expanding your knowledge.

Career teachers have very little reason to leave the classroom. They do not expect to be "promoted" into other jobs thus they have no reason to do anything that they do not think is best for their students. It is only those teachers who are having difficulty in the classroom that have to do thing to please administrators so that they can be "promoted" to a non-teaching job.

The years fly by and you have taught over a thousand students, over five thousand if you are in high school. You have laughed and learned everyday with your students. You have touched and been touched by many students. You have changed the lives of many of your students and through them have been a positive influence in our world. What job could have been better?

You have discovered the secret of a great life. You found something that you like, at which you are really good at and you can make a living doing it. Teachers are constantly looking for new things and ideas to bring to their students. When they are on vacation, they do not get email or messages from clients or the office about problems. What they bring back from vacation often ends up in their classroom or is integrated into their teaching.

Most teachers hate to miss a day of school. They go in when they are not feeling well rather than allow a substitute teacher to "cover" their class. Schools that allow teachers to accumulate their allotted "sick" days find many senior teachers accumulate years of sick leave by the time they retire. This has become an issue in many teacher union contracts. School districts do not want to pay teachers for accumulated leave but find a policy of "use it or lose it" hurt staff morale.

Many teachers only get "sick" on "in-service" days. Teachers who call in sick on an in-service day will often tell colleagues that they needed a "mental health day." When in-service days are scheduled on a Monday or Friday, the amount of teacher sickness soars. Now most schools hold their in-service days in the middle of the week. Parents find this very disruptive to their work schedule.

Teachers spend in-service days in meetings where they hear from the bureaucrats of their school districts about things that are important to bureaucrats, lawyers, and superintendents but these things usually have little to with helping teachers in the classroom. They also are required to attend workshops on educational methods lead by "educators" or "experts" who fled the classroom for one reason or another.[61] Teacher lead in-service days can be very useful and a lot of fun. Usually these in-service days occur near the end of the school year.

Teaching becomes easier with experience. At first you spent many hours mastering the subjects and planning lessons. Now you know the subjects inside and out. You have at least a half dozen ways to explain every idea or concept. You can sprinkle your lesson with jokes or puns, at will, to keep students attention. You have stories, trivia, and little known facts to make the subjects more alive to students. You have activities for every concept. You have kits of simple materials to enrich every lesson. You have a store of video to supplement lessons.

The first time you worked with a student whose family was breaking up, the student who was being abused, the student who was being bullied, the student who was suicidal, student deaths, etc. it was very difficult to know what to say or do. Now you have handled these and many other types of crisis many times. You have the experience to better guide students through their problems.

You have also had the joy of seeing your students find themselves, develop confidence and succeed in their endeavors. You can take pride in your students' successes. They become authors, actors, corporate executives, entrepreneurs, military officers, teachers, professors, lawyers, and doctors.[62] You may have one of your former students teaching in the classroom down the hall or have a child of a former student in your classroom now.

---

61 Remember Farber's fifth postulate: "Success in the teaching profession is not teaching."

62 I never had a student become an Indian chief. There is not much opportunity for that job on the east coast.

You became a master teacher. Any job that takes you out of the classroom is probably not a better job for you. It will not allow you to make
use of all the knowledge and skills that you developed for the classroom.
Taking a job out of the classroom is not a promotion, rather it is a career change. This is true even if the job comes with an increase in salary. It is a different job which will require different skills and knowledge.
If you decide to leave the classroom, there is no reason that you should
continue working in the educational system. A manager job is not really
much different whether it is in manufacturing, health, government or
education. The skill set needed to be successful is basically the same. The
same can be said for administrative jobs. If the reason that you choose to
leave the classroom is for a higher salary, consider business and industry.
They often pay more than school systems. There are greater opportunities
for advancement and promotion in industry. A company with an annual
profit and loss statement will permit you to demonstrate your value. This
is more difficult in education.

As a teacher, you get to continuously expand your horizons and
knowledge. You can follow your interests in summer graduate work,
workshops, travels and jobs. You are not locked in to any specific area. I
was able to expand my knowledge by taking courses in geology and me-
trology. I pursued my interest in genetics through workshops and courses. I spent a summer in a paid research program at a medical school,
trying to determine the gene site for malignant hyperthermia. Another
summer I worked in plastics research and helped develop a clear plas-
tic with a sun screen rating of 87. I went to space camp for teachers. In
a whale study, I had the thrill of being a mile off an Atlantic island at
midnight in a kayak surrounded by a pod of whales. I also drove trucks
and bulldozers. Another summer, I ran a dry cleaning facility. I spend
several summers supervising conservation projects for the U. S. Fish and
Wildlife Service.

A teacher can have a rich life, rich in many diverse experiences, skills
and knowledge. I know of no other job that allows as much personal

freedom for following and expanding your personal interests. Teachers are amazing people. A typical random group of school teachers will have more talents, diverse knowledge and experiences than most any other professional group.

—

Let's take a look at the job of school principal. Many teachers aspire to this position. From the spelling of the title, it means that this person is the *principal teacher* or the main teacher. I went to grade school in a building that had eight classrooms, four on each of the two floors and a kindergarten area in the basement. There were nine teachers. The sixth grade teacher, and the only male teacher, was the principal teacher. He had the keys to the store room. While I was too young to accurately observe all of his functions, I clearly remember that my teachers went to him for classroom supplies. I also remember that students who were really "bad" were taken into the supply room for "discipline." It was rumored that he kept a wooden paddle in the supply room. I didn't want to find out. Yes, times have changed.

Today a school principle does not teach classes. The duties of a principal have expanded into a job that has less to do with teaching and more with negotiating budgets, schedules, and personal. To obtain a principal's certificate in most states requires that a person complete a course of study which is similar to that an M.B.A. The principal reports to a superintendent who is a political appointee. The superintendent usually serves at the pleasure of an elected school board. In my state, the average superintendent serves only five years before moving on to another school district or job. With each change of superintendent, comes new directions, new programs, new curricula, different "standardized tests," all of which must be implemented by the principal.

Any successful principal could make much more money in business or industry.

—

So you are a classroom teacher, you are successful and love your job, but your paycheck isn't enough for the life style that you desire. What should you do?

First is to find a school that pays its teachers better. Don't stay in a school or school district in hopes that salaries will improve in the future. You will be told by the "powers that be" that things will get better. Politicians' promises don't pay bills. There is nothing more worthless than a politician's promise.

Don't wait too long. To change schools, you need to have less than five years teaching experience. Most schools prefer to hire teachers at the lower end of their salary schedule. The school may want a teacher with some experience but they also want someone who is not set in their ways.

Most schools will not hire a teacher with many years of experience unless they have some unique skill, attribute or fame. A teacher who is certified to teach many different subjects is more useful to a school than one with a doctorate. The more diverse the certifications, the more useful to a school. Often schools do not have enough classes to need a full time teacher in a particular subject. I remember working with a teacher who taught Spanish and math and another that taught English and biology. Some schools will hire a teacher because he or she has a record as a successful coach. Don't think that only physical educational teachers can coach. In my last school, the science teachers included the head football coach, the wrestling coach, the swimming coach, gymnastics coach and the softball coach.

You don't want or can't change schools for some reason or another. What do you do to increase your salary? There are several things to think about.

In every school there are a wide variety of extracurricular positions. These can be coaching positions, drama director, or sponsor of a student activity. There are other jobs such as running the school store, liaison to parent groups, recruiter, publicity director etc. These require extra time but provide an immediate increase in pay.

Look at the school's salary schedule. Teachers will receive an increase or "step" for each year that they teach in the system up to a certain number. There is no way to accelerate the years of experience steps. Look at the lateral steps for academic accomplishments. Salary schedules will increase with the number of graduate credits, with a master's degree and a doctorate degree. Some salary schedules will have an increase for multiple subject certifications. The advantage of moving laterally on the salary scale is that once you move, you will receive this higher salary for the remainder of your time in this school system. The disadvantage is that you must spend time and money and will not see any increase in pay until you reach the lateral step.

Some teachers keep adding to their academic accreditations until they can teach at colleges and universities. Many begin as adjunct professors teaching evenings or weekends before going full time. Today higher level institutions are using more adjunct professors than ever before.

Many teachers have started their own summer or part time businesses. Some offer employment to students in painting, lawn care, or catering. Others have started day camps that offer academic enhancement. Some teachers arrange trips and lead student groups as tour guides.

You may never get rich as a teacher but you can make a comfortable living. As you move up the salary scale things will gradually get easier.

CONCLUSION

Hopefully this little narrative has given you insights that will help you differentiate between that which you can change and that which you can not change. You now will not waste your time and energy trying to change things in the educational system that, in reality, can't be significantly changed. You will avoid being frustrated. You will be able to laugh at the things that frustrate teachers. Some other teachers will likely burn out trying to change the system. You may carry this book to facility meetings to protect and preserve your sanity. Remember that nothing you say or do in a facility meeting will get you a salary increase or bonus.

Life is too short to be taken seriously. You are a classroom teacher. That is what you trained for. You are comfortable and successful in the classroom. You laugh and learn with your students every day. You get to share their joys but also console and cry with them when tragedy strikes. What job could be better?

You can change the lives of your students and through them be a positive influence in our world. A hundred years from now no one will remember much about you. They will not remember the car you drove, your house or the size of your bank account. But the world may be different because of your influence on your students.[63]

---

63 Paraphrased from Forest Witcraft.

ABOUT THE AUTHOR

Robert Farber earned his undergraduate degree from Grove City College and his graduate degree from Temple University in Science and Education. He has spent more than forty-five years as a classroom teacher in some of the toughest schools in Philadelphia, as well as top-rated public and private schools, teaching all levels of students from middle school through college.

During summers he has completed additional coursework and continuing education workshops at the University of Maryland, Penn State University, Central Florida University, Bryn Mawr University, and Princeton University, covering such subjects as Brain & Behavior and Molecular Biology. His summer jobs have ranged from construction to genetics research.

Robert has served in many capacities with educational organizations, civic associations, and youth organizations. He is the author of *Off The Shelf Chemistry Laboratory Manual*. Now retired, Robert and his wife, Janice, enjoy traveling and camping.

CPSIA information can be obtained at www.ICGtesting.com
Printed in the USA
BVOW02s0002090615

403719BV00001B/16/P